D1083713

Ethical Principles
for
Social Policy

Edited by John Howie

Southern Illinois University Press
Carbondale and Edwardsville

Copyright © 1983 by the Board of Trustees,
    Southern Illinois University
Second printing, February 1984
Printed in the United States of America
Edited and designed by Dan Gunter
Production supervised by John DeBacher

Library of Congress Cataloging in Publication
    Data

Main entry under title:

Ethical principles for social policy.

    Bibliography: p.
    Includes index.
    Contents: The ethics of respect for life /
William K. Frankena—Zero population growth
and zero economic growth / William T. Blackstone—Racism, sexism, and preferential treatment / Richard Wasserstrom—[etc.]
    1. United States—Social policy—Moral
and ethical aspects—Addresses, essays, lectures.
2. United States—Moral conditions—Addresses,
essays, lectures.   3. Social ethics—Addresses,
essays, lectures.   4. Social values—Addresses,
essays, lectures.   I. Howie, John.
HN59.2.E35   303.3'72   82–5801
ISBN 0–8093–1063–5   AACR2

Dedicated to Helen Benson Leys
and
the memory of Wayne A. R. Leys

Contents

Contributors

William K. Frankena, Professor Emeritus, University of Michigan, has enriched philosophical discussions as the author of six books, including *Ethics* (1963), *Some Beliefs About Justice* (1966), and *Thinking About Morality* (1980), and as the Carus lecturer (1974), "Three Questions About Morality." He is the author of more than 100 articles, many of which have appeared in important edited collections. Goodpaster, one of his students, calls Frankena's work in the field of ethics "a model for philosophical methodology" since it combines historical sensitivity, analytical precision, and normative emphasis with a balanced "philosophical restraint."

William T. Blackstone, Jr., former Research Professor of Philosophy at the University of Georgia, is the author of *The Problem of Religious Knowledge* (Prentice-Hall, 1963), *Francis Hutcheson and Contemporary Ethical Theory* (University of Georgia Press, 1965), and *Political Philosophy: An Introduction* (Harper, 1973), and is editor or co-editor of seven books, including *The Concept of Equality* (1969), *Meaning and Existence* (1971), and *Philosophy and Environmental Crisis* (1974). He is also the author of more than sixty articles. His last writings deal most explicitly with the application of moral principles to such problems as discrimination, health care, environmental issues, and population growth.

Richard Wasserstrom, Professor of Philosophy and Chairman of the Philosophy Board at the University of California, Santa Cruz, holds degrees in both law and philosophy. He is the author of *The Judicial Decision* (1961), and, most recently, *Philosophy and Social Issues, Five Studies* (1980), and is editor of *War and Morality* (1970), *Morality and The Law* (1971), and *Today's Moral Problems* (1975). Having served as an attorney for the Civil Rights Division of the Department of Justice, he can speak from first-hand acquaintance with racism and sexism.

Gerald Dworkin, Professor of Philosophy at the University of Illinois, Chicago Circle, is the author of the widely influential essays "Paternalism," "Acting Freely," "Reasons and Authority," and "Autonomy and Behavior Control." He is editor of *Determinism, Free Will and Moral Responsibility* (1970), and co-editor of *Ethics* (1968), *The I Q Controversy: Critical Readings* (1976), and *Markets and Morals* (1977).

Joel Feinberg, Professor and Head of the Philosophy Department, University of Arizona, has written extensively in the fields of law, philosophy, and ethics. He is the author of *Doing and Deserving: Essays in the Theory of Responsibility* (1970), *Social Philosophy* (1973), and *Rights, Justice and The Bounds of Liberty* (1980), and editor of *Reason and Responsibility* (1965), *Moral Concepts* (1970), *The Problem of Abortion* (1973), *Philosophy of Law* (1975), *Moral Philosophy* (1977), and *Philosophy and the Human Condition* (with Beauchamp and Blackstone, 1980). One of his fields of special interest is the interlocking of morality and law and their bearing on the life of the individual and society.

Tom L. Beauchamp, Professor of Philosophy and Senior Research Scholar at the Kennedy Center for Bioethics, Georgetown University, is the author of *Philosophical Ethics* (1982), and co-author of *Principles of Biomedical Ethics* (with James Childress, 1979), and *Hume and the Problem of Causation* (with Alexander Rosenberg, 1981). He is editor of *Philosophical Problems of Causation* (1974) and *Ethics and Public Policy* (1975), and co-editor of *Thomas Reid: Critical Interpretations* (1976), *Contemporary Issues in Bioethics* (1978), *Ethical Issues in Death and Dying* (1978), *Ethical Theory and Business* (1979), and *Philosophy and the Human Condition* (1980). In his recent work Beauchamp has addressed such prominent issues in bioethics as autonomy, informed consent, euthanasia, genetic intervention, right to health care, and paternalism.

Acknowledgments

ENCOURAGEMENT, HELP, AND FINANCIAL SUPPORT from a number of persons have made this volume possible. For assistance with proofreading I am indebted to John C. Belcher, Jerome Carpenter, William Frey, Brian Mahalick, Mario Sáenz, Bruce Smith, and Stephen Timpe. Angela B. Rubin of Morris Library unselfishly and cheerfully gave her time to complete and correct a number of important notes, and Ann Puckett of the Law Library assisted with the legal citations. The Philosophy Department and its chairman, Professor James A. Diefenbeck, Dr. Michael R. Dingerson, Associate Dean of the Graduate School and Director of Research Development and Administration, and Dean James F. Light of the College of Liberal Arts, Southern Illinois University, provided both encouragement and financial support at crucial stages. Helen Benson Leys offered suggestions and generously paid the necessary expenses of bringing the manuscript to final form.

For permission to reprint Professor William K. Frankena's essay "The Ethics of Respect for Life," I am grateful to The Johns Hopkins University Press; the essay was initially published in *Respect for Life in Medicine, Philosophy and The Law*, edited by O. Temkin and others (1977). Mrs. William T. Blackstone has kindly given permission to publish her deceased husband's lecture, printed here for the first time. Professor Peter A. French, editor of *Midwest Studies in Philosophy* (University of Minnesota Press), has given permission to publish Professor Gerald Dworkin's paper "Is More Choice Better Than Less?" which will appear in Vol. 7 of that series (1982). Professor Wasserstrom has granted permission to publish his paper, "Racism, Sexism, and Preferential Treatment: An Approach to the Topics," which had been published (in somewhat different form) in *University of California* (Los Angeles) *Law Review* 24 (1977): 581–622. Professor Joel Feinberg's essay "The

Child's Right to An Open Future" was published initially by Littlefield, Adams and Company, in *Whose Child? Children's Rights, Parental Authority, and State Power*, edited by William Aiken and Hugh LaFollette (1980). It is reprinted with permission.

For the final typing of the manuscript I am grateful to Deborah Brockmeyer and Virginia Johnson.

John Howie
Carbondale

Introduction
The Wayne Leys Memorial Lectures

EVEN LEAVING ASIDE HIS EARLIER ACCOMPLISHMENTS and service, the contributions of Wayne Leys as a scholar, professor, and valued colleague at Southern Illinois University, Carbondale, would require special acknowledgment and praise. Lewis E. Hahn, a colleague, has appropriately described him as a cooperative and creative person who, from a generous store of knowledge and a fertile mind, had something to contribute on a wide range of problems. A person of courage and conviction, he would not sidestep controversy when principles were threatened. He added a significance to the common efforts of the philosophy staff, and his example of quiet reasonableness, especially in times of stress and difficulty, continues to provide both encouragement and direction.

Having joined our staff in January, 1964, Leys worked selflessly for the department and his many students, graduate and undergraduate, until his death March 7, 1973, at the age of 67. In a joint effort with S. S. Rama Rao Pappu, a student from India, Leys prepared the centennial volume *Gandhi and America's Educational Future* (Southern Illinois Univ. Pr., 1969). This inquiry is a reflection of Leys's open, experimental, and truth-seeking spirit.

It was, of course, only one of the nine books he wrote. Three earlier books, *Ethics and Social Policy* (1941), *Ethics for Policy Decisions* (1952), and *Philosophy and the Public Interest* (with Charner Perry, 1959), all reflect Leys's major concern to relate ethics to public policy. Leys conceived of such policy as including all significant decisions made by politicians, administrators, judges, lawyers, and ordinary citizens. His purpose was to bring the deliberative ethical questions to bear on the exciting and complicated issues of social policy for the sake of a balanced, reasonable judgment.

Leys believed that philosophy should be part of the fabric of public policy and personal decisions. In particular he was persuaded that contemporary social controversies contained implicitly the perennial questions of philosophical ethics and that ethics has relevance and importance for every discussion of social policy. One of his lifelong endeavors was to make ethical principles and ethical criticism accessible and intelligible to people who evaluate public policy and personal plans. Typically, Leys would begin a discussion with a current social controversy and then show (often with a touch of dry humor) how the approach and teachings of Socrates, Aristotle, Kant, Marx, and Dewey could help one formulate the salient ethical features of the puzzle and could stimulate further thought. He knew that such controversies were the natural frames for philosophical interests and that probing questions, more often than flat answers, serve as Socratic midwife to creative personal growth and independent development of ideas.

To continue this salutary emphasis, the Leys family and many friends, in cooperation with the Southern Illinois University Foundation and the Department of Philosophy at Southern Illinois University, Carbondale, have established the Wayne Leys Memorial Lectureship Fund. Money from its endowment provides each year for a special lecture by an outstanding philosopher chosen by the Department. The first six of these lectures are gathered in this volume. In their stress upon the application of ethics to social policy, they mirror a major interest and characteristic turn of thought of Leys himself.

In the opening essay Frankena asks how respect for human life affects policy decisions involving the preventing or shortening of human life. The answer hinges in part upon whether one takes a comprehensive or noncomprehensive view of life. If "life" refers to human bodily life, it needs to be distinguished from personality, and respect for human bodily life will not be the same as respect for personality. Violations of respect for human bodily life may not necessarily involve violations of respect for personality. Frankena also notes that respect for human bodily life is essentially moral rather than religious. However, this respect is a derivative and qualified principle; thus, although it is always wrong presumptively, *ceteris paribus*, or prima facie to shorten or prevent a human life, it is not always actually wrong to do so because other moral considerations may counterbalance the presumed wrongness.

While Frankena offers an individual approach, Blackstone invites us to consider the twin macro-problems of zero population growth and zero economic growth in terms of the ethical principles of freedom, social welfare, and justice. Population size and its exponential growth make disturbingly clear the gravity of the current threat. If such growth continues at the same rate as in the past, then by the year 3520 A.D. the weight of the human species will exceed that of the planet itself and each person (if the land were divided equally) would have less than one square foot of land. To these staggering physical results must be added the even more ominous social consequences: more crime, more malnutrition, and more starvation. Are not stringent population controls already necessary (at least in some countries) for maximizing freedom, human welfare, and social justice? From whatever value framework the needed coercive population controls may be applied, it is important to insist that, in addition to technological changes, attitudes, norms, and incentives also be altered.

The value principles connected with zero economic growth appear even more problematic. Taking Mancur Olsen's real per capita income as the most reliable indicator of social and economic welfare, Blackstone assesses the advantages and disadvantages of zero economic growth. The limited capacity of the ecosystem to absorb waste and the threat of uncontrolled growth to the supply of non-renewable, non-reproducible natural resources and to the performance of essential functions such as nutrient cycling, climate regulation, and pest control indicate that in the near future a no-growth economy may be necessary for survival. But for the present, at least in the United States, a no-growth approach seems to be an oversimplification. The planning and control for such an extreme approach would, in any circumstances, have to be international. Moreover, a no-growth policy would have detrimental results for distributive justice, fostering a greater inequality of family incomes. The wiser course, it would seem, is controlled economic growth.

Wasserstrom focuses on the widespread economic and social inequities of racism and sexism. As social realities, race and sex affect both the way the individual looks at the world and the way the world looks at the individual. To be black, for example, is to be considered different from and inferior to the adult white male; it is to be a member of a disliked and oppressed minority. In an even more radical way differences in sex role are reflected in differences in socialization. People are taught to see men as independent, capable, powerful; women are considered dependent, limited, and passive. Sexism seems to be a more serious problem than racism since it is less visible, harder to eradicate, and to some at least, less unequivocally unjustifiable. Wasserstrom insists that only the assimilationist ideal of a nonracist and nonsexist society allows the individual to develop his or her characteristics, talents, and capacities in accord with purpose and desire.

In his essay Gerald Dworkin examines critically an assumption underlying many social policy debates and decisions. He considers the proposition that for the rational individual more choices are always preferable to fewer. This assumption, common to economists as well as political philosophers of different persuasions, has been used to justify inheritance of wealth and to support a form of income redistribution. Dworkin offers conspicuous exceptions to this assumption where the additional choices and their costs reflect either general features of choice or intrinsic features of particular choices. Among these exceptions are decision-making costs, enlarged responsibilities, situations decreasing the likelihood of previous choices and limiting future choices, increased choices that result in loss or decline of welfare, and paternalistic circumstances where a wider range of choice increases the likelihood of choosing contrary to one's own best long-range interests.

How does one assess social policy concerning children? Feinberg offers an answer by considering children's "rights-in-trust" which compose what he calls "the right to an open future." This right may be violated by others before the developing person achieves the ability to exercise it through choice. It sets limits on the ways which parents may raise their children and imposes duties on the state as *parens patriae* to enforce those limits. The grounds of these duties are self-determination (autonomy) and self-fulfillment. The state may justify its interference with parental liberty by holding that the right of self-determination is violated in advance whenever parents make momentous and irrevocable decisions determining the course of the child's life before the child has the capacity for self-determination. In a parallel manner, the state may be warranted in interfering when parental actions prevent the child from developing his major aptitudes into genuine talents and from realizing the human propensities to design, plan, and make order.

A concluding essay by Tom Beauchamp deals with the relation

of medical paternalism to voluntary action and comprehension. Paternalism has been the basis for courts ordering blood transfusions when patients have refused them, for committing persons to mental treatment against their wishes, and for resuscitating patients who explicitly asked not to be resuscitated. In general, paternalism as a moral problem involves interference with a person's freedom of action or freedom of information for reasons referring exclusively to the welfare, good, happiness, interests, or values of the person interfered with. As one liberty-limiting principle, it needs to be distinguished from others such as the offense principle, the welfare principle, and the harm principle. An examination of the arguments offered by paternalists and antipaternalists suggests that there is a common ground between them. The justification for intervention seems to rest not upon different views of liberty-limiting principles but rather upon different theories of voluntariness and information possession.

According to both paternalists and their opponents, temporary intervention on behalf of patients is morally appropriate in situations where we are unsure whether a person's actions are sufficiently voluntary or his judgment is adequately informed. In more difficult cases, where actions are only partially voluntary or only partially informed, the harm principle could be extended to apply. Protection of patients from harm resulting directly from their uremic condition, pain, retardation, or drunkenness would be morally permissible. As soon as adequate information was acquired and voluntariness restored, intervention would no longer be morally allowable. The desirable perspective for many of these cases would draw together a philosophical account of the nature of voluntary and cognitive abilities with an empirical account of the impairment or disability of voluntariness and comprehension.

These essays invite the reader to discover the relevance of clearly stated, balanced, and reasonable ethical principles to controversial issues of our time. Expressing insights not warped by emotionalism, yet sensitive to deeper feelings and intuitions, they are sure to capture attention, provoke reflection, and generate discussion.

John Howie
Carbondale

Ethical Principles
for
Social Policy

I

The Ethics of Respect for Life
William K. Frankena

EXPRESSIONS LIKE "RESPECT FOR LIFE," "reverence for life," and "the sanctity of life" have a currency today they never had before. Outside of Schweitzer, whose writings are recent, they occur mainly in discussions of a family of topics now very much in both the public and the philosophical eyes, topics grouped together under such headings as medical ethics, bioethics, environmental ethics, or ecoethics. They serve, somewhat vaguely and ambiguously, to identify a concept or group of concepts—or rather, a doctrine or group of doctrines—that are central in those discussions. The point is that many of those who take conservative positions on the matters referred to are appealing to what they call "respect for life," "the sanctity of life," and so forth, and regard their opponents as denying this. As one of them put it on television not long ago, "Until recently we believed life to be a sacred value, now we do not." It is my purpose to say something about this doctrine from a philosophical point of view, and I propose to be partly historical and partly systematic, since my interests run both ways and may be combined. What I hope to do is to provide some help in our thinking on relevant topics, which is at present a kind of potpourri of ideas and theses partly historical and partly logical or philosophical. I shall begin by introducing some distinctions and definitions that seem to me necessary for understanding and discussing them.

RESPECT FOR LIFE: DISTINCTIONS AND DEFINITIONS

We are talking about "respect (or reverence) for life" and "sanctity of life." These two and similar phrases recur in relevant discussions, and I shall use them more or less interchangeably. If one has respect for life, one believes life has sanctity, and vice versa.

If one believes we should respect life, one believes in the sanctity of life, and vice versa. But now, as Socrates might ask, what does the word "life" refer to in this context? In bioethical discussions, it is usually used to refer to human life, but, of course, it may also be used to refer to life in general, life of all kinds, and is so used in ecoethical discussions, which are part of what we are interested in here. Accordingly, I shall divide our subject into two parts: the topic of respect for human life, or life in human form, and that of respect for life as such or life in all its forms. I shall call the latter *comprehensive* respect for life and the former *noncomprehensive* respect for life. Let us take the former—respect for human life—first.

Even in this, the simpler case, the denotation of "life" is not entirely fixed, and concern for life may mean concern for each individual life or concern for the life of the human species. Tennyson recognized this when he said of Nature (felicitously but unhappily), "So careful of the type she seems,/ So careless of the single life. . . ."[1] Between these two kinds of concern for life, there may also be concern for the life of one's lineage and of one's tribe or race. Here, I shall be interested primarily in concern for the individual life, since this seems to be what is central in bioethics, but I shall also refer on occasion to the other types of life. Even in the case of the individual, we can speak of his bodily or physical life and of his mental life, and in some views, the latter may have begun before the former and go on longer, perhaps even eternally, either in a disembodied way or in another body or a resurrected one. I shall take it that what is primarily in question here is the former, and so ordinarily we mean by "life" the sort of bodily thing possessed by us between conception or birth and death. It is clearly life of this sort that is prevented or taken in abortion, contraception, euthanasia, suicide, and the like.

There have been many metaphysical views about what human life in this sense involves—naturalism, supernaturalism, dualism, materialism, idealism, epiphenomenalism, transmigrationism, behaviorism, and the identity theory. Some of these views have been used to support, and others to refute, a belief in the sanctity of human life. I shall, however, refer to them only occasionally, my general feeling being that such metaphysical positions are less relevant

1. *In Memoriam,* LV.

to our ethical issues than is often thought. I am not sure that any of them are incompatible with a belief in the sanctity of human life, except perhaps those, if any, that deny the existence of consciousness or of such experiences as pleasure, pain, happiness, suffering, hope, and despair.

We must make more distinctions in the meaning of life at this point. First, we must distinguish between respect for human life in the biological sense just defined—that is, respect for existence as a living human organism—and respect for human individuality or personality. I say this because some writers—for example, Hans Jonas[2]—seem to equate the sanctity of human life and the sanctity of human individuality or personality. But being an individual or person and having personality include much more than being alive, and one may have respect for individuality, personhood, or personality without having respect for life as such, and vice versa. Somewhat more carefully, Edward Shils says that "three forms of life" are referred to in "the postulate of the sanctity of human life": the life of the lineage, already referred to; the life of the human organism, which I am taking as central; and the life of the individual as an individual "possessing consciousness of itself as an agent and patient both in the past and the present." "The sanctity of the individual," he says, "is a variant form of the sanctity of life." Thus he regards concern about what he calls "contrived intervention" as concern for the sanctity of life, including concern not only about abortion and artificial inovulation but also about genetic engineering, medical modification of personality qualities, and "intervention . . . into the islands of privacy which surround individuality."[3] This is, explicitly or implicitly, a rather common view, but it does involve giving a very extended sense to the terms "life" and "respect for life" and covers up the fact that abortion and personality modification, euthanasia and invasion of individuality, are very different things, one involving the taking of what is usually called life and the other not. It seems to me better to notice clearly and to under-

2. Cf. Hans Jonas, *Philosophical Essays* (Englewood Cliffs, N.J.: Prentice-Hall, 1974), pp. 12, 17, 107, 163. For a good corrective argument see J. G. Milhaven, *Toward a New Catholic Morality* (Garden City, N.Y.: Image Books, 1972), p. 225.

3. "The Sanctity of Life," in *Life or Death: Ethics and Options*, ed. Daniel H. Labby (Seattle: Univ. of Washington Pr., 1968), pp. 29 ff., 32, 8–10.

line this difference and to speak of concern for life in one case and for individuality or personality in the other. Not all the moral problems of medicine are questions about the sanctity of life, and some of the rights discussed go beyond those recognized in respect for life, at least in the sense in which I mean to understand it here.[4] It still may be, of course, that human life should be respected only or partly because it is a seat for individuality or personality; but that is another matter.

In a somewhat similar way, we must distinguish concern about *quantity* of life in the sense of concern about the length of an individual's life or about the number of individual lives (such as is involved in discussions of abortion, suicide, contraception, war, human sacrifice, and population control), from concern for the *quality* of life and for improving it (such as we hear so much about in discussions of ecology and the environment). Concern for the quality of life is not strictly concern for life but for something else— goodness of life, freedom of life, or the like. One may seek to reduce differences in the quality of life to differences in quantity, as Herbert Spencer tried to do by talking about differences in the "breadth" or fullness of life, and then defining this in terms of quantity or change packed into a given time, but this is not very convincing, as Spencer himself in effect admits when he says his view presupposes that conduct which promotes "the greatest totality of life" also promotes pleasure or happiness.[5]

The Meaning of Respect

Now that we are reasonably, though not entirely, clear what respect for human life is respect for, namely bodily life, what *is* respect for life? I assume that the desire to live is basic to man— that, although they may come to reject life and risk it every day, people do normally want to go on living. If altruistic, they may also desire that others live longer and that there be more of them. But such love of life and of the living is not respect for life; in Kant's terms it is "pathological," for it does not include any normative or value judgment about its object as such. To respect life is to believe in the sanctity of life, and this entails making some kind of normative or value judgment about it, not just feeling or acting in a cer-

4. See, e.g., Jonas, *Philosophical Essays*, p. 163.
5. See Herbert Spencer, *The Data of Ethics* (New York: A. L. Burt Co., n.d.), chap. 2, para. 9.

tain way toward it.[6] Desiring or loving something does not by itself include making any such judgment; though it may generate such a judgment, that judgment is not simply an articulation or report of mere desire or love.[7] What kind of a normative or value judgment is involved in respect for life? It might be a judgment of admiration, of aesthetic appreciation, or of cognitive curiosity—of what C. I. Lewis called "inherent value"[8]—like "Life is beautiful." I think we generally do have such aesthetic or cognitive interests in contemplating life; even if we do not find it all admirable or beautiful, we do tend to find it interesting. And, indeed, in the discussions relevant here, there do sometimes appear quasi-aesthetic expressions like "human dignity," "the dignity of the individual," and the "dignity" or "integrity" of human life.[9] It is then, however, usually clear that "dignity" does not have a merely esthetic meaning, and that the concern in such contexts is not just esthetic or contemplative, but ethical.[10] Respect here is not just a kind of admiration or curiosity; it may actually contain no admiration or curiosity at all.

It may be thought that respect for life is or includes a judgment of value that is not esthetic but also is not moral—for example, a judgment like "Life is good" or "Life is worth living." In fact, excepting maybe Rousseau and Bret Harte, none of us believe that human life is morally good, for this would be to believe that there are no bad people. But it is often held that life is good or worth living in either an instrumental or an intrinsic way, though pessimists have sometimes denied this. Thus, in *The Morals of Evolution*, M. J. Savage maintained that "life . . . is worth living for itself alone,"[11] and somewhat earlier Robert Browning wrote these lines: "How good is man's life, the mere living! How fit to employ/All the heart and the soul and the senses for ever in joy!"[12] These verses,

6. Cf. R. S. Downie and E. Telfer, *Respect for Persons* (London: Allen and Unwin, 1969), p. 18.

7. See my "On Saying the Ethical Thing," *Proceedings and Addresses of the American Philosophical Association* 39 (1966): 21–42.

8. See his *Analysis of Knowledge and Valuation* (La Salle, Ill.: Open Court, 1946), p. 360.

9. Cf., e.g., Jonas, *Philosophical Essays*, pp. 17, 107, 180; Labby, *Life or Death*, pp. xviii, 58, 71.

10. Cf. Jonas, *Philosophical Essays*, p. 107.

11. M. J. Savage, *The Morals of Evolution* (Boston: G. H. Ellis, 1880), p. 22.

12. *Saul*, IX.

which make it sound as if all human life were like the beginning of *Oklahoma*, are contradicted by what happens later in that same poem. In any case, those who believe in the sanctity of life in our context are not holding that life is good in itself in this way; they may do so, of course, but they hold that even if or when it is not, human life still has sanctity in their sense. Indeed, it is doubtful that anyone ever really believed that life is good in itself, no matter how qualified, even if it is painful and vicious, even if it is unconscious and contains no pleasure or pain, hope or fear, aspiration or achievement. Certainly, to assert the sanctity of life is not just to assert that it is good as a means to something else; it is true that life is, at least while we are on earth, a necessary condition of our enjoyment or achievement of value or disvalue, and because it is, perhaps we should ascribe sanctity to it, but to say life is necessary is not automatically to ascribe sanctity to it. Ascribing sanctity to life is not just judging that it is worth living as a means or an end in itself; it is more like judging that one living being should respect other living beings. So, once again, what is respect for human life?

Two rather different answers have to be distinguished. One is to say that human life is sacred, sacrosanct, or even holy; the other is to say that live human beings have certain rights, that it is wrong to treat them in certain ways. These two lines of thought are often confused or conflated, but, even if the first entails the second, they should be distinguished. It seems to me that the doctrine of the sanctity of life takes two rather different forms: a religious or protoreligious form in which it is natural to speak of respect for human life as including awe for it, and a more purely ethical or moral form in which it is not natural or at least not necessary to do so. The first, of course, is maintained by many religious thinkers—for example, Karl Barth, Paul Ramsey, and Hans Jonas.[13] Interestingly, however, it is also maintained by the social scientist Edward Shils, who regards it as "self-evident" that life is "sacred" and thinks that its sacredness is so basic and primitive as to be presupposed both by the religious and by the ethical beliefs in the sanctity of human life.

> The source of the revulsion or apprehension [about "contrived intervention"] is deeper than the culture of Christianity . . . [in]

13. Cf. Ramsey, "The Morality of Abortion," in *Life or Death*, ed. Labby, pp. 74 ff.; Jonas, *Philosophical Essays*, pp. 179 ff.

a deeper, protoreligious "natural metaphysics." . . . The chief feature of [this] is the affirmation that life *is* sacred. It is believed to be sacred not because it is a manifestation of a transcendent creator . . . [but] because it is life. The idea of sacredness is generated by the primordial experience of being alive, of experiencing the elemental sensation of vitality and the elemental fear of its extinction. Man stands in awe before his own vitality, the vitality of his lineage and of his species. The sense of awe is the attribution and therefore the acknowledgment of sanctity . . . the transcendent sacred is a construction which the human mind itself has created to account for and to place in a necessary order the primordial experience. . . . If life were not viewed and experienced as sacred, then nothing else would be sacred. . . .

[Is] human life really sacred? I answer that it is, self-evidently. Its sacredness is the most primordial of experiences . . . the task for our generation and those immediately following is not so much the reestablishment of . . . Christianity . . . but rather the rediscovery of . . . the protoreligion, the "natural metaphysic" of the sanctity of life.[14]

The second form of the doctrine of respect for life is, or at least may be, held independently of religion in anything like its traditional forms. It is also possible for one to subscribe to the doctrine in both forms, without holding that the second depends on the first; it may be that Ramsey and Jonas do this—they do implicitly distinguish the religious and the moral forms of the doctrine—but they still regard the second as in some way inadequate.[15] More typically, theologians, especially Protestant and Jewish ones, have held that the religious form of the doctrine both entails and is presupposed by the moral form. They also typically claim, as we shall see, that the moral doctrine of the sanctity of life emerged historically from the Judeo-Christian religion, and even that it would not have appeared if that religion had not entered the world.

Shils's position is interesting here, for he holds that the moral view depends on the religious, both historically and logically (if I understand him), but denies that it depends, either historically or logically, on "the culture of Christianity and its doctrine of the soul" or on any traditional religious belief or faith. I cannot try

14. Jonas, *Philosophical Essays*, pp. 9, 12 ff., 18 ff., 38.
15. Cf. Ramsey, "The Morality of Abortion," pp. 70 ff.; Jonas, *Philosophical Essays*, pp. 19 ff., 179 ff.

to assess his views here, though I think they should not simply be brushed off. But even if Shils is correct in his historical thesis, it seems certain, as we shall see, that Judeo-Christian religious beliefs did play a large role in the emergence of the moral form of respect for life. In any case, it seems to me that for us, in connection with the problems of bio- and ecoethics, the crucial form of the doctrine of the sanctity of life is the moral one, and that any religious form of the doctrine is of interest only if it is presupposed, historically or logically, by the moral one. In short, I take respect for human life, in the sense in which we are concerned with it, to involve the making of a specifically moral judgment about such life (not just a value judgment of some other sort, religious or nonreligious); that is, it involves saying that certain attitudes toward or ways of treating human life (bodily life) are morally good or bad, right or wrong. I am supported in this by a feeling that judgments of sacredness, awesomeness, holiness, etc., are more like esthetic ones than like moral ones, and a consequent doubt that they are presupposed by moral judgments (rather than the other way around).[16]

It should be observed that "human life has sanctity" (or "is to be respected"), in the sense in which we shall take it here, actually means that it is morally wrong to treat human life in certain ways; therefore, one cannot sensibly say that it is wrong to treat human life in these ways *because* human life has sanctity, for this will be a mere tautology.

UNQUALIFIED AND QUALIFIED RESPECT

We must make even more distinctions. So far I have been arguing that we should take as central the idea of moral respect for quantity of individual human bodily life—that is, the idea that some or all acts reducing the quantity, either duration or number of such bodily life or lives are morally wrong. We must now notice, first, that such acts are of two kinds: acts of ending or shortening a human bodily life—for example, killing, suicide, and euthanasia; and acts of preventing possible human bodily life—for example, contraception (even rhythm), sterilization, celibacy, and refraining from sexual intercourse. Acts of abortion will fall under either

---

16. I shall continue to use the expression "sanctity of life," but only in the moral sense just indicated.

heading—under the first if fetuses are human beings, as Ramsey and others think, under the second if they are not, as still others think. By unqualified respect for human life (or belief in the sanctity of human life) I shall mean the view that all acts of either kind are wrong, absolutely or *ceteris paribus*; by qualified respect for human life, the view that some or all acts of the second sort are permissible or right but acts of the first sort are wrong, at least prima facie in W. D. Ross's sense.[17]

As was just implied, each of these views can be held in either of two ways: one may hold that the sanctity of human life is absolute in the sense that it is never overruled by other considerations—that it is always actually wrong to end or prevent a human life; or one may hold that it is not absolute—that it is always wrong presumptively, wrong *ceteris paribus*, or prima facie wrong, to shorten or prevent a human life, but not always actually or finally wrong, since other moral considerations may still make it right in certain circumstances. For example, in the famous case in which a choice must be made between killing a fetus and allowing both fetus and mother to die, the first view will choose the latter alternative, and the second the former. Both views subscribe to the sanctity of human life, but in different ways; both regard killing the fetus wrong as such, but the second view holds that its wrongness is overridden by the fact that otherwise both fetus and mother will die, while the first view denies this. The fact that a belief in the sanctity of life can take these two forms is important to remember, for it is often assumed—by our television speaker and by William Temple and J. F. Fletcher in the argument to be discussed later, for example—that those who believe in the sanctity of human life must hold that it is absolute and inviolable, and that those who hold it to be sometimes right to end a fetal or human life do not believe that it has any sanctity. Even Henry Sidgwick makes this assumption.

My final distinction may be introduced as follows. Belief in the sanctity of human life may simply mean belief that abortion and other acts of the kinds just listed are morally wrong, either absolutely or prima facie. This seems to be what W. E. H. Lecky and Ludwig Edelstein mean in the discussions we shall review shortly.

17. Cf. W. D. Ross, *The Right and the Good* (Oxford: Clarendon Pr., 1930), pp. 19 ff.

However, like Socrates, we must ask here what makes these actions wrong, what they have in common, and the answer must be that they are wrong because they involve the shortening or preventing of a human bodily life. Otherwise, no respect for human bodily life as such is at issue. For example, if it is held that such acts are wrong because they are forbidden by God, no doctrine of the sanctity of bodily life is implied, unless it is added that God forbids them as acts of shortening or preventing such life. But even if such acts are taken to be wrong, absolutely or *ceteris paribus*, as acts of shortening or preventing human bodily life, they may be taken to be so in different ways. If we ask what makes acts of shortening or preventing human bodily life wrong, then one answer is to say that such acts are wrong just because they are acts of ending or preventing a human bodily life. In this view (and only in this view), the sanctity of human life, absolute or presumptive, is a basic ethical principle, holding that we should respect human bodily life as such, because of what it is and not because of other facts about it. The other answer is to say that human bodily life is to be respected (or has sanctity) not because of what it is but because of other facts about it—such as that it is accompanied by consciousness, is a condition of intellectual or moral perfection, or is loved or valued by God. In this second view, the sanctity of human life, whether absolute or presumptive, is a derivative ethical principle, based on a prior principle to the effect that we should respect consciousness, seek perfection, or love what God loves. In both views, the sanctity of human physical life is maintained, but only in the first is it held to have sanctity as such. In other words, in the first view such life is respected directly, as such or for its own sake; in the second it is respected indirectly, for the sake of something else— consciousness, perfection, or God. The latter view is that life has a kind of sanctity all right, but not simply as life; in this sense only the first view entails a straight-out respect for life.

SANCTITY OF HUMAN LIFE IN HISTORY

These distinctions made, let us look at the history of the idea of the sanctity of human life. The television speaker quoted earlier said we used to believe that life has sanctity, but that today we do not. This statement is inaccurate: we never all believed that life had sanctity even in the moral sense, and some of us still do. What is true is that not long ago, abortion, suicide, and other such acts were much more generally proscribed in Western morality and law than they now are. It is also true that they were much less proscribed in ancient times than they were more recently. Indeed, we may say that, at least until lately, there was a gradual evolution of respect for human life in the moral and legal systems of the West— if not in the actual practice of Western man, then at least in his preaching, in his judgments about abortion, infanticide, human sacrifice, gladiatorial combat, murder, suicide, and war. One small sign of this is the way the use of the Hippocratic oath, so carefully studied by Edelstein, came to be an increasing part of the ethics of the medical profession, a story I will come back to. Most accounts of the development of our law and morality agree about this. The classical account is that of W. E. H. Lecky in his *History of European Morals* (1869), in which the expression "the sanctity of human life" was already (first?) used.

> Considered as immortal beings, destined for the extremes of happiness or of misery, and united to one another by a special community of redemption, the first and most manifest duty of a Christian man was to look upon his fellowmen as sacred beings, and from this notion grew up the eminently Christian idea of the sanctity of human life . . . nature does not tell man that it is wrong to slay without provocation his fellowmen . . . it was one of the most important services of Christianity that besides quickening greatly our benevolent affections it definitely and dogmatically asserted the sinfulness of all destruction of human life as a matter of amusement, or of simple convenience, and thereby formed a new standard higher than any which then existed in the world. . . . This minute and scrupulous care for human life and human virtue in the humblest form, in the slave, the gladiator, the savage, or the infant, was indeed wholly foreign to the genius of Paganism. It was produced by the Christian doctrine of the inestimable value of each immortal soul.[18]

Except for some more evolutionary writers, most historians of Western morals agree with Lecky that the rise of Judaism and especially Christianity, had a great deal to do with the growth of

18. W. E. H. Lecky, *History of European Morals from Augustus to Charlemagne*, 11th ed. (London: Longmans Green, 1894), II, 18, 20, 34. Also cf. Henry Sidgwick, *Outlines of the History of Ethics* (London: Macmillan, 1931), pp. 122 ff.

the "sense of the sanctity of human life"—that there was either little or no recognition of the sanctity of life in ancient pagan culture, and that any such recognition was either generated or greatly increased by the advent of the Judaic and Christian religions, through their doctrines of creation, the nature of God, ethics, the immortality of the soul, and the hereafter. It seems to me that this general picture is approximately correct. To complete it in the same rough global way, we may say, as was indicated, that this growth of the sense of the sanctity of human life has received a considerable check in recent decades, no doubt partly because of the decline and fall of the Judeo-Christian empire over our minds; but we must add that we are at the same time seeing a broadening of the notion of respect for life to include not just human or even animal life but also plant life and, indeed, all of nature—that is, what I called comprehensive respect for life, a broadening that seems to have no special ties with the Judeo-Christian tradition (though at least some thinkers in the tradition seem to favor it) and may be mainly influenced by romanticism, evolutionism, and Indian philosophy.[19]

This rather global picture cannot be fully documented here, but some comments and points, mainly historical, must be made. One can begin by asking whether there has been a growth of the sense of the sanctity of human life even within Judaism and Christianity. I am disposed to think there has been, though Lecky points out that proscriptions of some things like abortion, infanticide, and human sacrifice were part of Christianity from the very beginning; however, I shall not discuss this question.

More interesting is the question of the extent of the sense of the sanctity of human life in Western ancient pagan culture. In their apologetics, Judeo-Christian theologians sometimes minimize it, and it certainly is true that the Greeks and Romans (to say nothing of those they called barbarians) had less of this sense than the Christians, judging by their attitudes to abortion, etc. But, as Georgia Harkness says, there is a kind of respect for life in every society. "In every society there appears to be an elemental reverence for life which makes the deliberate killing of another person a punishable offense. In all societies there are exceptions . . . yet aversion to

19. Cf. Jonas, *Philosophical Essays*, pp. 10, 179 ff.; see also Schweitzer, *Civilization and Ethics*, 3d ed., and Joseph G. Brennan, *Ethics and Morals* (New York: Harper, 1973), pp. 337–44.

murder is probably the most universal of all moral attitudes."[20] As for abortion, etc., there was at least some disapproval of such kinds of action, and even some legal prohibition, in Greek and Roman society, as Lecky makes clear. It remains true that the idea of the sanctity of human life is far from complete even in the best pagan philosophers, if measured by their attitudes toward abortion, etc., or toward barbarians.[21]

Ludwig Edelstein's discussion of the Hippocratic Oath and the Pythagoreans, which has already been mentioned, is relevant here. Among other things, the oath, which he assigns to the fourth century B.C., includes the article which expresses a strong disapproval of abortion, euthanasia, and suicide, independently of Judeo-Christian influence. Discussing this clause, Edelstein contends that it did not reflect the general view (let alone the practice) of the physicians of Greece or Rome and was not subscribed to by physicians generally until "the end of antiquity"—until Christianity arose and became dominant—and that, in fact, it was not an expression of any prevailing Greek views, and long represented "a small segment of Greek opinion."

> Ancient jurisdiction did not discriminate against suicide; it did not attach any disgrace to it, provided that there was sufficient reason for such an act. And self-murder as a relief from illness was regarded as justifiable . . . in some states it was an institution duly legalized by the authorities. Nor did Greek or Roman law protect the unborn child. If, in certain cities, abortion was prosecuted, it was because the father's right to his offspring had been violated by the mother's action. Ancient religion did not proscribe suicide. It did not know of any eternal punishment for those who voluntarily ended their lives. Likewise it remained indifferent to foeticide. . . . Law and religion then left the physician free to do whatever seemed best to him.
>
> From these considerations it follows that a specific philosophical conviction must have dictated the rules laid down in the Oath. Is it possible to determine this particular philosophy? To take the problem of suicide first: Platonists, Cynics, and Stoics can be

20. *The Sources of Western Morality* (New York: Scribner's, 1954), p. 24.

21. Cf. Lecky, *History of European Morals*, II, 17–61, and Edelstein as cited next. Here and in what follows I use "abortion, etc.," as short for "abortion, euthanasia, contraception, suicide, etc."

eliminated at once. They held suicide permissible for the diseased. Some . . . even extolled such an act as the greatest triumph of men over fate. Aristotle . . . and Epicurus [were opposed to suicide but this] did not involve moral censure. If men decided to take their lives, they were within their rights. . . . The Aristotelian and Epicurean schools condoned suicide. Later on the Aristotelians . . . under the onslaught of the Stoic attack [even] . . . withdrew their disapproval of self-murder . . . indeed among all Greek thinkers the Pythagoreans alone outlawed suicide and did so without qualification . . . the same can be asserted of the rule forbidding abortion. . . . Most of the Greek philosophers even commended abortion. For Plato, foeticide is one of the regular institutions of the ideal state . . . Aristotle reckons abortion the best procedure to keep the population within the limits which he considers essential for a well-ordered community.[22]

Edelstein then recognizes that Aristotle and later Greek philosophers held that abortion is permissible only before the fetus attains the state of "animated" life, but adds that they did not hold that animation begins at conception but somewhat later, or not until birth. Then he says, "It was different with the Pythagoreans. They held that the embryo was an animate being from the moment of conception . . . [and] could not but reject abortion unconditionally." He further contends that this article, and the oath generally, must be regarded as an expression of the Pythagorean philosophy and/or religion of the fourth century B.C., which did prohibit abortion and suicide, and in general held to a very rigorous regimen, wishing thereby to reform both medicine and life.

I have a feeling that, to make his case for the Pythagorean origin of the oath, Edelsetein slightly understates the extent to which the other ancients disapproved of abortion and suicide. Still, his general line of argument is convincing, and, while it does establish that Pythagoreanism was an exception to the usual picture described earlier, it also makes clear that Pythagoreanism was the kind of exception that helps to prove the rule envisaged in that picture. One may doubt, however, that the Pythagoreans really did regard life as having sanctity as such. Whether or not they did depends on their reasons for proscribing abortion and suicide. Their argument against

22. For my references to Edelstein, see *Ancient Medicine: Selected Papers of Ludwig Edelstein*, ed. Owsei Temkin and C. Lilian Temkin (Baltimore: Johns Hopkins Pr., 1967), pp. 6, 14 ff. and *passim*.

suicide, Lecky and Edelstein agree, was "that we are all soldiers of God, placed in an appointed post of duty, which it is a rebellion against our Maker to desert,"[23] but, while this shows that they saw sanctity in duty or in God's ordering of things, it hardly shows that they believed in the sanctity of life itself, of the union of body and soul that constitutes a human being. Moreover, if the Pythagoreans believed in the transmigration of souls and in the associated notion of the body (*soma*) as the tomb (*sema*) of the soul from which it seeks to escape, as Burnet and others hold they did,[24] then they can hardly have believed in the sanctity of bodily life as such, even though they regarded suicide as absolutely wrong. As for abortion, Edelstein says that the Pythagoreans had to proscribe it because they considered it a man's duty to beget children so as to leave behind him more worshipers of the gods,[25] which hardly suggests that they proscribed it out of a respect for life as such; but he also says that they had to regard abortion as murder because they maintained that one is a living being, uniting body and soul, from the moment of conception on, which would suggest that they did respect life as such, if they did not also hold to the *soma-sema* doctrine or appeal to the principle that one must not interfere with God's schedules of arrival and departure. The Pythagoreans believed in a qualified respect for life, apparently as an absolute principle, but probably regarded it as derivative from some more basic consideration and not as ultimate.

In connection with Christianity, as well as with paganism, one may ask whether its opposition to abortion, etc., entails its being committed to the sanctity of bodily life as such. It does, if one simply means by belief in the sanctity of life, belief that abortion, etc., are wrong.[26] As we saw, however, whether or not one believes in the sanctity of bodily life as such depends on one's reasons for regarding it as wrong to shorten or prevent such life. We may, then, ask why Christianity regards this as wrong.

The usual answer is to say, as Lecky does, either that the human

23. Lecky, *History of European Morals*, p. 43; Edelstein, *Ancient Medicine*, p. 17.

24. Cf., e.g., John Burnet, *Early Greek Philosophy*, 3d ed. (London: A. C. Black, 1920), pp. 277 ff., but also 295.

25. Edelstein, *Ancient Medicine*, pp. 18 ff.

26. As R. C. Mortimer does, *Christian Ethics* (London: Hutchinsons' Univ. Library, 1950), chap. 8.

soul is immortal or that it is immortal and therefore has "inestimable value." But this reply will not do the job, because, as we just saw, one might hold that the body is a tomb from which the soul seeks to be free; from a soul's immortality or inestimable value it does not follow that it is wrong to prevent or break up a union of body and soul. Another answer is to say that man is to be respected because he was created in the image of God, but again it is not clear that this by itself means that we should respect each union of soul and body as wrong to interfere with, especially since God is immaterial. A third reply is to argue that after God had created man by shaping a body and infusing it with a soul, he looked at the result and "saw that it was good," indeed "very good."[27] Assuming that this was true and remained true after the Fall, I am once more not sure the wanted conclusion follows. For the judgment that the creation was good can hardly be a moral judgment and would seem to be esthetic or quasi-esthetic in the sense mentioned earlier; such a judgment would then not necessarily entail, without further ado, that it is morally wrong to kill any creature, plant, animal, or human, as the sequel in Genesis seems to show.

A better answer than these is to say that we are to respect human life because God does—because He loves His creatures, or because He commands us not to kill ourselves or others and to love our neighbors as we love ourselves. This line of thought is stressed by Paul Ramsey: "The value of a human life is ultimately grounded in the value God is placing on it. . . . [A human being's] dignity is 'an alien dignity,' an evaluation that is not of him but placed upon him by the divine decree [or by the act of divine love]."[28] As Ramsey notes, however, this approach does not ascribe intrinsic value to a human life; it makes the sanctity of such a life dependent on its relation to God, not on "something inherent in man." In this sense, it does not entail a belief in the sanctity of human life as such— that is, a belief that preventing or shortening a human union of body and soul is as such wrong either *ceteris paribus* or absolutely.

To this, of course, a Christian may reply, "So be it! All that matters is that preventing and shortening human lives are morally wrong; whether they are morally wrong as such or not is unimportant." This may be, but then at least we must be clear just what we

27. *Genesis* I.
28. Ramsey, "The Morality of Abortion," pp. 72–74.

are claiming if we claim that life has sanctity and on what ground. In any case, we may note that at least two Christians reject the belief that "physiological life" has sanctity, whether intrinsically or otherwise. Joseph Fletcher quotes with approval the following from William Temple: "The notion that life is absolutely sacred is Hindu or Buddhist, not Christian. . . . [The] belief that life, physiological life, is sacrosanct . . . is not a Christian idea at all; for, if it were, the martyrs would be wrong. If the sanctity is *in* life, it must be wrong to give your life for a noble cause as well as to take another's. But the Christian must be ready to give life gladly for his faith, as for a noble cause. Of course, this implies that, *as compared with some things*, the loss of life is a small evil; if so, then, *as compared with some other things*, the taking of life is a small injury."[29] If Temple and Fletcher are right, then the idea of the sanctity of life is not a Christian concept and we must look elsewhere for its source— perhaps in romanticism, evolutionism, or Oriental thought. However, Temple and Fletcher show at most that Christianity does not entail that it is always actually wrong to shorten a human life—or to give one up—and this is compatible with holding that it is always presumptively or prima facie wrong, or wrong other things being equal, to do so. It may then still be that Christianity does essentially assert the sanctity of human life at least in this sense, and I believe it does, but my question is, "Why? On what grounds?" I have argued that some of the usual replies will not do, or at least will not serve to show human life (bodily or physiological) has sanctity or should be respected as such.

Yet one more reply of this sort is to argue that it is wrong for anyone to end the bodily life of anyone else, or even of himself, because what happens to one in this life determines what future his soul will have in the hereafter. For example, it has been held, according to Lecky, that if one kills an animated fetus, one is dooming a soul to hell forever, since it will then perish without having been baptized.[30] Granted the premises, such reasoning does show that bodily life is of crucial importance and that ending it may be wrong, but it does not show that it is wrong as such, or even that it is wrong under all circumstances.

29. J. F. Fletcher, *Morals and Medicine* (Princeton: Princeton Univ. Pr., 1954), p. 193.
30. Lecky, *History of European Morals*, p. 23.

There is, however, another line of thought in Christianity. In rejecting the body-soul dualisms of the Pythagoreans, Platonists, and Gnostics, including the *soma-sema* conception of human life, Christian thinkers have often insisted on the unity and goodness of man's nature as a combination of body and soul, citing, among other things, the doctrines of the Incarnation and of the resurrection of the body as supporting such a view.[31] They use this line of thinking to show that the body is not inherently bad and to provide a basis for rejecting asceticism, but not to establish the sanctity of the life of each soul in its body (that is, the wrongness of preventing or shortening it), although obviously the argument may be used to show this too. But it still leaves open the question of whether human bodily life has moral sanctity as such or only because of some relationship in which it stands to God.

Some kind of belief in the sanctity of human life, though not necessarily in that of life in the body as such, is involved in the long tradition that evolved among Catholic philosophers and theologians out of Aquinas's discussion of self-defense—namely, the tradition that centers on a distinction between what one intends or directly wills and what one permits and only indirectly wills, together with the so-called doctrine of double effect. As I understand it, writers in this tradition at first applied this distinction and doctrine to self-defense, capital punishment, and war, as well as to other issues. They were in effect taking it as an absolute principle that it is always wrong intentionally to take a human life—whether it be as an end or as a means to some other end—the life of an assailant, criminal, or enemy soldier, as a means to saving one's own, protecting society, or defending one's country. All that is morally tolerable in this view is permitting people to die as an unintended (though foreseen) side effect of what one does in order to achieve some end other than their death. This position is hard to defend when the people in question are attacking one's life or country, and not unquestionable even when they are guilty of murder. As a result, the tradition referred to has tended in more recent times to apply its distinction and doctrine only in conflict cases in which the life of an innocent human being is at stake. That is, it tends now to posit only the absolute sanctity of innocent and noncombatant human lives, and to apply the principle of double effect,

31. Cf., e.g., George F. Thomas, *Christian Ethics and Moral Philosophy* (New York: Scribners, 1955), p. 159.

not in cases of self-defense and the like, but in cases involving abortion, euthanasia, suicide, self-sacrifice, judicial murder, sterilization, contraception, etc.

This shift involves moving to a somewhat limited, though still absolute and very significant, principle of respect for life. The principle is limited in two ways: first, in the way just indicated, by a kind of denial of the sanctity of the lives of certain criminals and combatants, or at least by a belief that they have in some way forfeited or exempted themselves from the right not to be killed as means to an end other than their death (for it is still regarded as absolutely wrong to take even their deaths as an end); and, second, in another way, by the assertion that while it is wrong or intolerable to take an innocent life intentionally even as a means, it is not always wrong voluntarily to "let die," that is, to do something (perhaps an "act of omission") which has the result that innocent people die.

The core of this traditional Catholic position is the doctrine of double effect, the main thrust of which, for present purposes, is that it is always morally intolerable or wrong to take an innocent human life intentionally, either as an end or as a means to some other end, however good; but that it is sometimes morally permissible voluntarily to let fetus or innocent person die—namely, when nothing evil is taken either as an end or as a means and when permitting the death is justified by "proportionate reasoning" of considerable weight. Applied to the crucial case already mentioned, this doctrine implies that it is wrong to kill the fetus in order to save the mother, since to do so is to *intend* its death as a means to one's end, and that it is right to *permit* both to die even though one could save the mother. On the basis of this and other cases, as well as on other grounds, many recent Catholic writers are giving up or modifying the traditional position, especially the principle that it is absolutely wrong to bring about the death of a fetus or innocent person intentionally, no matter what the alternative may be.[32] Perhaps some of them are also giving up the belief in the sanctity of human life. But this does not follow; one can reject the tradition and still believe that it is always prima facie wrong either to kill an innocent person or to let one die voluntarily.

I said that the tradition in question believes in an absolute but

32. See Richard A. McCormick, *Ambiguity in Moral Choice*, Pere Marquette Lecture, 1973; and Milhaven, *Toward a New Catholic Morality*, pp. 128 ff., 225 ff.

limited kind of sanctity of human life. This does not mean that it believes, even in this limited way, in the sanctity of human bodily life as such. Whether it does or not depends on why it regards the taking of an innocent life as wrong, and it may answer this question in different ways—for example, by saying that it is wrong because it is against God's law. It need not say, and may or may not hold, that it is wrong just because it is the shortening of the bodily life of some human being.

It is, therefore, clear that Pythagoreanism played a small part, and the Judeo-Christian tradition a large one, in the evolution of the view that abortion, etc., are morally wrong, but it is rather less clear that they generated the idea of the sanctity of human bodily or earthly life as such. If they did not, where might this idea (if it is around at all) have come from? As was intimated, it may be a product of such more or less opposite movements as the Renaissance, romanticism (including Hegelian Idealism), and evolutionism. These movements certainly did bring about some new ways of speaking about life, or rather Life, the kind of talk about life that we sometimes find in Dewey and Whitehead—for example, the idea that life has no aim beyond itself, no end except more life, that education is life and life is the subject matter of education, and so on.[33] Commenting forcefully on this development of "vitalism" and its "eulogistic use of the word *life*," Morris Cohen wrote:

> That the continuance of mere physical life is an absolute moral good seems to be axiomatic in current ethics. It serves as a basis for the unqualified moral condemnation of all forms of suicide and euthanasia . . . this setting up of mere life as an absolute moral good . . . is inconsistent with the moral approval of the hero or the martyr who throws away life for the sake of honor or conscience . . . we cannot . . . dispense with the classical problem of defining the good and discriminating it from the evil of life. . . . Instead of life we want the good life. . . . Conduct, science, and art . . . depend on rational discrimination. . . . The essence of the romantic use of the [term] *life* . . . is that it avoids this necessary task.[34]

33. For an example of such talk see Jonas, *Philosophical Essays*, p. 13. I should also call attention to interesting historical remarks about "the modern life philosophy" by Hannah Arendt, *The Human Condition* (Garden City, N.Y.: Doubleday, 1959), pp. 285 ff., 375 ff., *passim*.
34. M. R. Cohen, *Reason and Nature* (New York: Harcourt, 1931), pp. 451, 457.

Actually, Cohen confuses somewhat the view that mere life is good and the view that it is absolutely wrong to end or give up a life. He also obscures the fact that those who adopt the evolutionary or romantic view of life are not typically against abortion, euthanasia, or population control. Still, he does put his finger on a kind of "worship of mere life" that does not stem from either classical antiquity or Christianity. It stems, in fact, at least partly from the evolutionism that arose in the nineteenth century, which did ascribe a kind of sanctity to life, human or nonhuman, by taking life as the end or good, and conduct as right or wrong according to whether it promotes or opposes life—one's own or life in general. As Sidgwick puts it, "Life (without breadth) is the ultimate end which certain writers of the evolutionist school are disposed to lay down instead of Happiness."[35] One must, however, be careful in interpreting evolutionary writers. Herbert Spencer appears to do this sort of thing when he writes, ". . . the conduct to which we apply the name good, is the relatively more evolved conduct . . . evolution becomes the highest possible when the conduct simultaneously achieves the greatest totality of life in self, in offspring, and in fellow men . . . [and] the conduct called good rises to the conduct conceived as best when it fulfills all three classes of ends at the same time."[36] But, as Sidgwick points out, "Substantially Mr. Spencer gives the most decided preference to 'pleasure' over 'life' as ultimate end. Immediately after the passage before quoted, which seems to take conduciveness to 'totality of life' as the criterion of 'good' conduct, he says there is an assumption involved in this view— namely that such conduct bring a 'surplus of agreeable feeling.' . . . He is therefore 'an Evolutionist Hedonist, not an Evolutionist pure.'"[37]

Discussing the pure "nonhedonistic" view that "Life (without breadth) is the ultimate end," Sidgwick argues, first, that "an ethical end cannot be proved by biology"; second, that the fact that we must live in order to live well "does not make life identical with living well"; third, that such prohibitions as that of killing or suicide are not self-evident but, so far as rational, rest ultimately on utilitarian grounds; and, fourth, that Spencer was right in "sub-

35. Sidgwick, *The Ethics of T. H. Green, H. Spencer, and J. Martineau* (London: Macmillan, 1902), p. 144.
36. Spencer, *The Data of Ethics*, p. 27 ff. Cf. pp. 51, 61, 70, 81.
37. Sidgwick, *Ethics of T. H. Green*, pp. 145 ff.

stantially" equating the good with pleasure rather than with life, since life may be painful and so is not desirable as such, but only when it is pleasant: "I quite admit that . . . part of the function of morality consists in maintaining such habits and sentiments as are necessary to the continued existence, in full numbers, of a society of human beings. . . . But this is not because the mere existence of human organisms, even if prolonged to eternity, appears to me in any way desirable it is only assumed to be so because it is supposed to be accompanied by Consciousness on the whole desirable; it is therefore this Desirable Consciousness which we must regard as ultimate Good."[38]

However this may be, it should be emphasized that even when those who hold this evolutionary view have taken life to be the ultimate end, they have not typically drawn the conclusion that abortion, etc., are morally wrong. The view has, therefore, not tended to support the pro-life movement that has recently been lobbying for this conclusion, even though it has generated a kind of regard for Life.

While Sidgwick was attacking naturalistic ethics of a vitalistic kind, he did so without any reference to Judeo-Christian doctrines or to religion or supernaturalism of any kind. Indeed, his discussion emphasizes the fact that, at least in British moral philosophy, questions relating to the sanctity of life (while not raised in those words) had long been debated in very different terms. Roughly, the issue as he and his colleagues saw it was this: are any principles pertaining to the prevention or shortening of human bodily life self-evident or deducible from others that are self-evident, or are such matters to be determined entirely by considerations of utility, by considerations relating to one's own good or happiness or to that of the world? That is, the basic debate, as Sidgwick's review of the "methods of ethics" shows, was between deontological intuitionism and teleologism, either egoistic or utilitarian (that is, universalistic). This was the secular and philosophical form that the discussion took for those who held ethics to have a "bottom"—independent of revelation or of the special doctrines of the Judeo-Christian religions—many of whom were divines and counted themselves as Christian: the Clarkes, Samuel and John, Berkeley, Butler, Price,

38. Sidgwick, *Ethics of T. H. Green*, p. 144; *The Methods of Ethics*, 7th ed. (London: Macmillan, 1930), pp. xxxii, 355 ff., 396 ff.

and Paley, for example. Some believed in the sanctity of life in the sense of believing that certain sorts of treatment of life are self-evidently or demonstrably wrong as such, if not absolutely, then at least when other things are equal; the others (including Sidgwick) denied it in the sense of holding that such treatment is right or wrong depending on whether or not it is to one's good or to that of the world. Outside of theology, among moral philosophers this is essentially the form in which the debate goes on today, though with less reliance on intuition and self-evidence. It may even be, then, that the idea of the moral sanctity of human life really appeared not with Christianity but with the modern moral philosophers, so much influenced by the Stoics, who held "these truths to be self-evident." At any rate, this idea is nicely exemplified by Samuel Clarke when he writes, "it is without dispute more fit and reasonable in itself that I should preserve the life of an innocent man . . . or deliver him from any imminent danger, though I have never made any promise so to do, than that I should suffer him to perish, or take away his life, without any reason or provocation at all."[39] This does not say that suffering an innocent person to perish, or even taking his life, is always absolutely wrong, nor does it say that innocent life has sanctity simply as life, but it does proclaim the prima facie wrongness of taking an innocent person's life or of letting him die, and proclaims it as self-evident without any religious premises.

Here I should mention Kant, who, though not an intuitionist, was a deontologist and did proscribe murder and suicide on a priori and nonreligious grounds. His arguments in his later works are well known. Earlier, in his *Lectures on Ethics*, he said as a preface to his discussion of suicide:

> In fact, however, our life is entirely conditioned by our body, so that we cannot conceive of a life not mediated by the body and we cannot make use of our freedom except through the body. It is, therefore, obvious that the body constitutes a part of ourselves. If a man destroys his body, and so his life, he does it by the use of his will, which is itself destroyed in the process. But to use the power of a free will for its own destruction is self-contradictory. If freedom is the condition of life it cannot be employed to abolish

39. In. D. D. Raphael, ed., *British Moralists, 1650–1800* (Oxford: Clarendon Pr., 1969), 1:194.

life and so to destroy and abolish itself. To use life for its own destruction, to use life for producing lifelessness, is self-contradictory.[40]

Though against suicide, Kant did not regard preservation of one's life as one's highest duty; it may, he thought, be morally necessary to sacrifice one's life to avoid violating another duty, but doing this is not suicide. Thus he accorded bodily life a kind of sanctity independent of any divine command and of any immortality the soul may have. It is also clear, however, that what bothered him was not the thought that in suicide one is using one's bodily life as a means to its own destruction, but the fact that bodily life is a necessary condition of our life in the sense of the use of our will or freedom, and that, therefore, in committing suicide, one is using one's will or freedom as a means to its own destruction. Bodily life for Kant (here) has sanctity, but only indirectly, because it is necessary for the life of the will.

Of course, one may argue that, historically and causally or genetically, the Christian religion was necessary as a precondition of such views as Clarke's and Kant's, and this may be true. It still may be true, however, that those views are logically independent of any religious beliefs—as Clarke and Kant thought they were.

But whether fairness is a duty independent of utility or not, we must be fair (even) to the utilitarians and point out that while they deny that abortion, etc., are wrong simply as such, even they do or can subscribe to the sanctity of human life in at least two ways. First, in a way, they are inheritors of the Christian ethics of love (as the deontologists are inheritors of the ethics of the Ten Commandments). They insist that each and every person affected—or even each and every sentient being—is to be considered when we are trying to determine what is right and what is wrong: to this extent at least they may and do regard it a prima facie wrong to harm any such being or to take its life when no greater good is to be gained by doing so. Second, although an act utilitarian can regard rules prohibiting abortion, etc., only as rules of thumb arising out of previous calculations, a rule utilitarian may regard rules relating to the sanctity of life in a stronger light. As the example of Berkeley shows, a rule utilitarian may even believe in absolute,

40. Immanuel Kant, *Lectures on Ethics*, trans. Louis Infield (New York: Century, 1930), pp. 147 ff.

exceptionless rules.[41] That is, he may argue that, for the general welfare, it is necessary that we all accept and conform to certain prohibitions taken to have no exceptions, and, further, that among those prohibitions are those that forbid the preventing or shortening of human life. Such a line of argument, whatever its plausibility, would, if successful, establish the sanctity of human life—in the sense of establishing the principles that abortion, suicide, killing, etc., are wrong—on a utilitarian basis. It would, of course, not show that preventing or shortening human lives is always wrong (even prima facie) as such, but it would yield the same practical conclusions.

It may be asked whether anyone has actually denied that human life has moral sanctity, directly or indirectly, at least in some qualified and prima facie sense. The answer is that some social-contract theorists have denied or would deny this—namely, those who hold that we have no moral duties toward those who do not or cannot (for example, animals) enter into the relevant social contract with us, or that such persons and beings have no moral rights in relation to us. This position was taken by Hobbes and, possibly, by Rousseau.

WRONGNESS OF PREVENTING OR SHORTENING HUMAN LIFE

My discussion of the idea of respect for human life, except for some opening distinctions, has thus far been historical. Now I should like to say something systematic, by way of indicating some of my own views. The main question is: what, if anything, makes it wrong, at least presumptively, to prevent or shorten a human life? There are a number of possible lines of reply, some religious, resting on specifically religious premises, and some not. We cannot answer that what makes it wrong is the fact, if it is a fact, that human life has sanctity (or dignity, intrinsic worth, etc.), since this is a tautology. However, we can say, first of all, that what makes shortening or preventing human bodily life wrong is simply the fact that it is bodily life of a certain sort, that human bodily life has sanctity as such or in itself; and, in saying this, we may hold that this is so either because bodily or physical life has sanctity as such or because human physical life has. If one holds the former, one is holding that "x is (or will be) living" entails "It is wrong, at least prima

41. George Berkeley, *Passive Obedience*, 1712.

facie, to end or prevent its life," or, in other words, that plant and animal life also have sanctity—thus raising the question of comprehensive respect for life, which we will come to. If one holds the latter, one is believing that it is wrong to check, end, or prevent human bodily life, not just because it is bodily life but because it is human. Then we may ask what it adds to say that it is human, and I assume that the reply cannot be merely that it takes the form of a featherless biped or laughs. The reply must mention some essential, inherent, or intrinsic feature of human beings other than mere physical life. This could be the fact that they are conscious, have feelings, or whatever, and then it would imply that some nonhuman animal life has sanctity and should be respected too; or it could be the fact that human beings have reason, purposes, ambitions, hopes, and ideals, or that their souls are immortal. Just what one would mention here depends on what characteristics one regards as inherent in man, and this varies from view to view, especially from naturalistic to supernaturalistic ones. The point, however, is that if one takes this present line, then one is saying that what gives human life sanctity is not the fact that it is life but the fact that it is human—the fact that it is accompanied by rationality, moral capacity, immortality, or whatever is supposed to be distinctive of human beings. And then one is not believing in the sanctity of physical life as such, but in the sanctity of rationality, morality, immortality, or whatever. One may still believe that it is wrong, at least prima facie, to prevent or shorten a human life, but only if one also holds that doing so interferes with, puts an end to, or otherwise adversely affects someone's rationality, moral capacity, immortality, or whatever, not just because it affects someone's life. One would, then, be hard put to show that it would be wrong, even prima facie, to end the life of a human being who has become completely and incurably comatose.

Perhaps I should remark here that I do not see how merely being immortal would confer sanctity on human life. Would a redwood tree (*Sequoia sempervirens*) have sanctity if (or only if) it were to live forever if not cut down? More important, however, is a further point: if one believes that the human soul is immortal, and hence that its (spiritual) life cannot be ended by killing the body it may be in, then it becomes harder, not easier, to prove that it is wrong to kill that body. For then one must show that killing that body will adversely affect the soul's destiny in the hereafter or that it countervenes a divine ordinance, and these are things it is not easy to show, things which it may be necessary to take on faith, and which may therefore reasonably be doubted.

A second kind of answer to the question of why it is wrong to end or prevent a human life is to say that what makes it wrong is not any feature inherent to such life but some extrinsic or relational fact about it—for example, that it contributes to the perfection of the universe or to the glory of God, or that it stands in some other relation to God, such as that of being loved by Him. In such views it will be wrong, perhaps absolutely wrong, to prevent or shorten a human life, not because this is in any way wrong as such, but only because it entails interfering with the perfection of the universe, with something God loves, and so on. If human life does not stand in such relations, there would be nothing wrong in blocking or ending it.

A third possibility is that one might argue that what makes it morally wrong to block or end human life is the fact that it is intrinsically good in a nonmoral sense or sacred in the special sense mentioned earlier. I myself doubt, however, that human life is always or necessarily good in itself (unless this means only that it is prima facie wrong to interfere with it), and also that its being good in itself is a necessary condition of its being wrong to block it or end it. As for its being sacred, if this means something different from its being wrong to block or end it, then I doubt that this is either a necessary or a sufficient condition of its being morally wrong to prevent or shorten a bodily life. In any case, we still have the further question of what makes such a life good or sacred, and then the answer must take either our first or second lines, and has, in effect, been discussed.

I shall not further discuss views claiming that some religious premise is a necessary or sufficient condition of a belief in the moral sanctity of human bodily life. Such premises may be necessary or sufficient for a belief in the sacredness of human life, but I am not convinced that they are even relevant to a belief that it is morally wrong to interfere with such life. Now let us look at what I call unqualified belief in the moral sanctity of human life—that is, the claim that every kind of preventing or shortening of bodily human life is wrong, either absolutely or prima facie (if intentional). I said I doubted that anyone has ever really held this, and now I want to add that it seems incredible. For it entails that it is at least prima facie wrong to block intentionally the starting or the fruition, not only of a nascent, but even of any possible human life. Strictly, it means that it is prima facie or absolutely wrong to refrain from sexual intercourse (or artificial insemination) whenever the opportunity presents itself, if the woman is capable of impregnation and the resulting child will be viable as a human. In fact, refraining will be actually wrong, if one hasn't anything better to do. Surely, "Be fruitful and multiply, and replenish the earth" never meant this. Even if one regards contraception and early abortion as wrong, what about rhythm, voluntary celibacy, or plain disinclination?

One might, of course, insist that it is always prima facie wrong not to start a possible human being on its way, but add that its wrongness is very easily outweighed by other considerations, maybe even by the fact that one would rather do something else. But then the idea of the sanctity of human life has very little if any substance left. In any case, however, it seems clear that an unqualified belief in the sanctity of human physical life as an absolute principle, always wrong to violate, is incredible. Let us then consider the more qualified belief that acts of ending such a life are morally wrong, prima facie or absolutely.

While I am not sure that or when a fetus is a human being or a person, I myself find it hard to deny that, since it is a nascent human being and person, it is prima facie wrong intentionally to destroy it or let it die.[42] I doubt, however, that this is true simply because the fetus is alive. But it seems clear to me that it is, at most, only prima facie and not absolutely wrong, though I do not believe that its prima facie wrongness is as easily outweighted or overridden as many recent defenders of abortion do. More generally, when I take the moral point of view, it seems to me clear that some kind of qualified respect for bodily human life is indeed called for, though not just because it is life. It is called for because human life normally is or can be so much more than just life, in ways in which floral and other faunal life is not and cannot be. That is, it is called for by the fact that, for human beings as we ordinarily know them, bodily life is a necessary condition of their being conscious, joyful,

42. Cf. Mary A. Warren, "On the Moral and Legal Status of Abortion," *Monist* 57 (1973): 59. This position is also hard to defend, however; see M. Tooley, "Abortion and Infanticide," and J. J. Thomson, "A Defense of Abortion" in *The Rights and Wrongs of Abortion*, ed. M. Cohen, T. Nagel, and T. Scanlon (Princeton: Princeton Univ. Pr., 1974).

happy, moral, religious, or fulfilled. This means, as I see it, that bodily life, even in the case of a human being, does not have sanctity as such, but only as a seat for the realization of something more. In this sense, respect for human life—for what I called quantity of bodily life—turns out to be based on concern about the quality of such life after all. It also follows, of course, that our respect for human bodily life is or should be indirect and derivative, rather than direct or basic. To this extent Morris Cohen was right. I do think, however, that the moral sanctity of human life is at least partly intrinsic, not because it is intrinsic to life but because it is based on some inherent feature of human beings; that is, I do not think it is based entirely on something extrinsic to them or relational, as Ramsey seems to think.

It does not follow from this view that abortion is not prima facie wrong, or that fetal life has no sanctity, for a fetus is, as such, on its way to being human. Nor does it follow that abortion is never right; it does seem to me, for instance, that it is not wrong to perform an abortion when the only alternative is to let both the mother and the fetus die. It also does not follow, of course, that animal life has no sanctity, since at least some animals are capable of something more than just being alive. It does, however, follow that it is not necessarily morally wrong, perhaps not even prima facie wrong, to end or let end the life of a person who has become hopelessly comatose, at least if it is done under certain conditions.

COMPREHENSIVE RESPECT FOR LIFE

Let us now take up respect for life in general—plant and animal as well as human—still meaning by "life" bodily or organic life. Earlier I called this *comprehensive* respect for life, the belief in the sanctity of all organic life on earth and elsewhere. One can believe in the sanctity of human life without believing in that of all kinds of life; indeed, historically, human life has long and usually been accorded a sanctity not accorded to plant or animal life. However, if one holds that all life has sanctity, absolutely or *ceteris paribus*, one must hold that human life has it, too. In fact, we saw that in one view, human life has sanctity because and only because it is a form of life, and that if one maintains this, then one is committed to comprehensive respect for life (or at least for animal life). We should also notice that respect for life can assume any and all of the forms taken by respect for human life: it can be religious or moral, qualified or unqualified, and so on. I shall assume that this is clear, and will not run through the various possibilities.

In the way of history I shall be brief. In the East, as Temple noticed, comprehensive respect for life was advocated long ago in Hinduism and Jainism, but in the West it is, I believe, a relative latecomer. Remember that love of nature, admiration of nature, and curiosity about nature need not involve any moral respect for nature or life in my sense, for it may be sentimental or, if not, purely esthetic, quasi-esthetic, or cognitive. At any rate, the Genesis view that God gave man "dominion over the fish of the sea, and over the fowl of the air, and over every living thing that moveth upon the earth" seems to have been dominant in the Judeo-Christian tradition, though it went together with a kind of respect for all of creation as the handwork of God and as something he saw to be "very good." Even so, one finds in that tradition some feeling that living things are not to be destroyed or even prevented from coming into being wantonly, for no reason at all, or only for pleasure. However, the Judeo-Christian tradition does not seem to insist that the reasons need to be very good; the Jains at any rate took a much more absolute view, insisting that the reasons are never good enough. Later, as Cohen points out, there was a kind of praise of life in some of the romantics, which he exemplifies by William James's remark about the then-new philosophy: "It lacks logical rigor, but it has the tang of life."[43] As we saw, there was also in the nineteenth century a kind of evolutionary ethics that took the promotion of life as the end by which right and wrong are to be determined: we are to do what most advances life in length and/or in breadth, in the individual, in the species, and/or in the world. In short, we are to act in accordance with the movement of the *élan vital*. There were also related "vitalistic" ethics or ethics of the "affirmation of life" of various sorts—in Fouillee, Guyau, Nietzsche, Euken, and maybe Bergson. I have suggested that these developments may have had a hand in the development of the idea of the sanctity of life, but I should again point out that they hardly tend to support any conclusion to the effect that abortion, etc., are all wrong, though they may be responsible for a eulogistic use of the word "life."

This is where I must bring in Albert Schweitzer's view, including

43. Cohen, *The Rights and Wrongs of Abortion*, p. 450.

his picture of the history of ethics.[44] It is well known that he advocated an ethic of reverence for life—not just human life but all life. He saw such an ethic as the culmination of a long debate involving three previous types of ethic: (1) the ethics of rational pleasure, which he describes as "egoistic utilitarian" and attributes to some ancients and some moderns; (2) the modern "social-utilitarian" ethics of altruism or self-devotion, at least partly due to Christianity; and (3) the ethics of "self-perfecting," active and/or passive, under which he places the various ethical theories of Plato, Aristotle, the Stoics, the Jewish prophets, the antiegoistic and antiutilitarian British moralists, Spinoza, Kant, Fichte, Schopenhauer, Nietzsche, the Hegelian idealists, and the Indians and "the great moralists of China."

All of these, he maintains, are inadequate in one way or another. The first cannot account for self-sacrifice, and he drops it from further consideration. The second and third each leave out and cannot generate what the other takes as central. But they may be combined in a certain way, which involves their becoming "cosmic" and "mystical" and yielding (somehow) his culminating fourth ethic, that of reverence for life, of "responsibility without limit toward all that lives." With this we finally come—at least in the West—to the full conception and ethics of the sanctity of all life, of comprehensive, unqualified, and, I think, direct respect for life. "A man is truly ethical only when he obeys the compulsion to help all life which he is able to assist, and shrinks from injuring anything that lives. He does not ask how far this or that life deserves one's sympathy as being valuable, nor . . . whether and to what degree it is capable of feeling. Life as such is sacred to him. He tears no leaf from a tree, plucks no flower, and takes care to crush no insect."[45]

More recently, as has been intimated, some such comprehensive ethic of respect for life (and/or nature) seems to be behind some of the thinking going on, not only in bioethics but also in what I called ecoethics.[46] In such views, most of our historical moralities

44. See Schweitzer, *Civilization and Ethics*, 3d ed. (London: A. C. Black, 1949), chaps. 19–22.

45. Schweitzer, *Civilization and Ethics*, p. 243.

46. Cf. Jonas, *Philosophical Essays*, chaps. 1, 8; Joseph G. Brennan, *Ethics and Morals* (New York: Harper, 1973), pp. 337–44; Holmes Rolston III, "Is There an Ecological Ethic?" *Ethics* 85 (1975): 93–109.

and systems of ethics have been grievously anthropocentric, as Schweitzer charged. Such views are, I believe, rarely religious in a traditional Western theistic sense; sometimes they are oriental in spirit, sometimes they are esthetic or quasi-esthetic in motivation, sometimes they are animistic in their conception of nature, and sometimes they stress the continuity of man, evolutionary and non-evolutionary, with the rest of nature. Jonas, one of the more interesting writers I have read in preparing this paper, is tempted by them in the course of his "reflections on the new tasks of ethics," and seems to be trying to find some support for them in the Jewish religion.

In the light of these historical remarks, together with those made earlier, it looks to me as if the idea of respect for life that underlies the "pro-life" movements in recent bio- and ecoethical discussions is really a loosely related family of ethical beliefs resulting from a confluence of a variety of sources: the Judeo-Christian religion, deontological moral philosophy, romanticism, evolutionism, and certain Oriental systems of thought. In particular, it looks as if three rather different kinds of respect for life are involved in those pro-life movements: a noncomprehensive one consisting of a belief that abortion, etc., are wrong, absolutely or presumptively; a comprehensive one that eulogizes Life but does not entail any such opposition to abortion, etc.; and another comprehensive one, of which Schweitzer is an example, that both reverences life and condemns abortion, etc., as wrong.

In the way of systematic discussion of this comprehensive respect for life, I must be even briefer. Leaving aside the question of respect for nature, let us confine ourselves to that of respect for life, floral and faunal. Then I stand ready to allow that some ways of treating animals that are capable of feeling fear and pain are prima facie morally wrong, and that there is something wrong with killing such animals for the fun of it. But I am not sure that it is wrong to prevent their coming into life or to shorten their lives when they do, at least if this is done without causing fear or pain and is of some good to us. I certainly do not see that we have any moral duties to animals that are not conscious of fear, pain, or pleasure, or to plants (even if talking to plants does help them flourish). Unlike Brennan, I have not come to recognize the "postulate," ethical or not, "that every living thing has a prima facie claim on life and that if we override that claim in a particular instance we should be able to justify our action by sound reasons."[47] In short, I see no sanctity in mere life, in life that is not at least capable of conscious aversion, desire, enjoyment, fear, relief, pain, satisfaction, or suffering—and rather little in life that is capable of these but incapable of thought, purpose, hope, regret, and the like. I am all for ecology, environmental quality, conservation, bird watching, and game refuges, but not because I think biological life has any moral sanctity as such, but only because birds and many other animals are capable of feeling and suffering, and because they and the rest of nature are esthetically, cognitively, instrumentally, and perhaps even emotionally and socially, valuable to beings like us.[48] Such considerations suffice to show that certain ways of relating to nonhuman nature are morally wrong, as ecoethical moralists wish to claim.

The most plausible basis for a comprehensive respect for life similar to Schweitzer's, to my mind, would be an animistic metaphysics of the Leibniz-Whitehead type. However, while I am not entirely unsympathetic with the idea of such a metaphysics, I am very dubious about the project of ascribing intrinsic value to lives or spirits that have no conscious experience whatsover; thus, I am also dubious about saying that morally, we ought or ought not to treat them in certain ways, let alone saying that they ought or ought not to treat each other (and us?) in certain ways. Much depends here on the amount of analogy with ourselves that one is willing to ascribe to such lives or spirits, and on the extent to which one is willing to stretch the categories of value and morality.

SUMMARY

I have now made a good many distinctions and perhaps some points, historical, analytical, or normative. Some of the main nonhistorical points may be summarized as follows:

1. The sanctity of bodily human life is not relevant to the discussion of all bio- and ecoethical questions, but only to those involving the preventing or shortening of human life. Others involve the sanctity of individuality or personality, or quality rather than quantity of life. The sanctity of bodily human life should be distinguished from that of individuality or personality, even if there is a connection.

47. Brennan, *Ethics and Morals*, p. 344.
48. I am left unconvinced, even by Rolston's eloquent and perceptive argument in his "Is There an Ecological Ethic?"

2. Mere life, whether that of a vegetable, animal, or human organism, has no moral sanctity as such, though it may have esthetic and other kinds of nonmoral value, and may be a necessary condition of consciousness, rationality, or morality.

3. Life has moral sanctity, but only where it is a condition of something more, as it is in humans, fetuses, and some animals.

4. This something must be something inherent—consciousness, feeling, reason—in such living beings, not something wholly extrinsic, such as being immortal.

5. Even then the moral sanctity of bodily human life is not absolute; it is considerable, at least from the moral point of view, but it is only prima facie or presumptive.

6. The only tenable view, then, is a derivative, qualified, and noncomprehensive ethic of respect for life.

I have not tried to prove these points but only to state them in such a way as to make them clear and convincing, and to provide a kind of history of the ideas involved in them. Three other remarks are necessary in conclusion. First, in the view just formulated, the principle of respect for life is not basic but derivative; it is, however, not just a maxim or rule of thumb such as an act utilitarian or situational moralist might take it to be. In any case, in order to solve any of the actual problems of medical or environmental ethics —for example, abortion or population control—one must do more than merely appeal to that principle. One must appeal to the full body of all relevant basic ethical principles, old or new, of which that of the sanctity of life is a corollary, and one must make use of all the available factual knowledge bearing on the problem. Second, I have talked as if saying that life has sanctity means only that it is wrong to treat it in certain ways. This can, of course, be expressed more positively by saying that it is right or obligatory not to treat it in those ways, or that people, fetuses, or whatever have a right to life, though one must use the right-to-life way of speaking with some care if one uses it at all. Can one put it yet more positively by saying that it is right or obligatory to treat life in the opposite ways, by lengthening or multiplying it? In some very qualified sense I think the answer is yes, but I leave this question open here. A yes answer would add another dimension to my ethics of respect for life, but it would not otherwise affect what I have said. Third, I have mentioned law, but have confined my discussion to moral questions. However, as indicated by Glanville Williams' title, *The*

Sanctity of Life and the Criminal Law, our subject comes up in the law also. Indeed, any system of law almost necessarily embodies and enforces at least a qualified respect for human life—for example, in proscribing certain forms of killing. It is then a very important question whether our law should permit abortion, euthanasia, suicide, the hunting of animals, or the trampling of plants. I assume that it must permit the eating of at least some plants and seeds, but for the rest I leave such questions open.

II

Zero Population Growth
and Zero Economic Growth
An Exploration of Some of the Value Questions

William T. Blackstone

MUCH OF THE PUSH, THOUGH NOT ALL, for zero growth—both zero population growth and zero economic growth—has come out of concern about the immense environmental devastation being wreaked by unbridled growth and its negative impact on the quality of human life today and in the future. Ecologists and environmentalists have sensitized us to the need to think holistically about the environment, to learn about the regulatory mechanisms in nature which are responsible for ecosystem homeostasis, and to take these factors into consideration in any actions which alter the environment. And the work of demographers, agronomists, and population ecologists, and the sheer fact of massive malnutrition and starvation in some parts of the world, are sensitizing us to the need to control effectively population growth and to strike a balance between the environment's productive capacities and the demands made on those capacities.

In order to avoid calamitous consequences for mankind, controls both on population growth and on environmentally-damaging economic growth will be required. The causal factors seem to fuel one another. Excessive population in a given area leads to ill-advised land-use in order to squeeze out maximum food and resource production for immediate use. But this often leads to deforestation, erosion, and desertification. This makes for poverty in the long-run, which in turn seems to increase the birthrate. And the cycle goes on.[1] There is no way, then, of completely separating the issues at

1. For detailed discussion of the cycle and the causes, see Erik P. Eckholm, "Losing Ground: Impinging Ecological Disaster," *The Humanist* 33 (Nov./Dec., 1973): 17-21.

stake in zero population growth from the issues at stake in zero economic growth, but, for the purposes of this paper, I want to treat them separately. This will, I hope, permit me to focus more specifically on the complex value questions involved in these two zero-growth movements and at least to point in the direction of a reasonable resolution of them. Consider, first, zero population growth.

ZERO POPULATION GROWTH

What are the facts cited by those who argue for zero population growth? What are the results to which they point if population growth is not controlled or reduced to zero? Is it necessary and desirable at this stage of human history for coercive measures to be used in order to limit population growth? If so, what should these measures be?

Arguments for compulsory population control

Here is the picture painted by those who press for coercive measures: It took the time-span from the Garden of Eden to 1830 A.D. for the human population to reach one billion. It took only a hundred years to add the next billion; only thirty years to add the next billion; and only fifteen years to add the fourth billion, bringing us to 1976. If we continue at this exponential rate, we will be adding a billion persons every five years at the turn of the century. We have been warned that if the present growth rates continue for 650 years each person alive will have less than one square foot of land to call his own, and by the year 3520 A.D. the weight of the human species will exceed that of the planet itself.[2] In fact, if zero population growth were attained in the developed world by the turn of the century and in developing nations by 2040 A.D., the population of the world would still quadruple to approximately 16 billion.

Advocates of zero population growth (ZPG) point to the staggering social and environmental implications of these figures. Under conditions of relative resource scarcity, there will be more crime, more malnutrition, more disease, mass starvation, and continual threats of war. It is estimated that 500 million persons today are

2. Message from the President of the United States Relative to Population Growth, July 21, 1969, H. R. Doc. No. 139, 91st Cong. 1st Session 3 (1969).

suffering and dying from malnutrition. The environmental degradation which accompanies population growth threatens the existence
of basic necessities, such as food, shelter, and water, not to speak
of those esthetic, recreational and cultural amenities which are essential to human well-being. Even the viability of democracy as a
form of government is threatened by population growth, as Aldous
Huxley and Robert Heilbroner have argued.[3]

Arguments against compulsory population control

Now this picture—both the population predictions and the social
predictions—are challenged by those who argue especially against
compulsory population controls. It is argued that we do not have
accurate figures showing the number of people now existing in the
world, that we have no reliable way of forecasting future population
growth, that there is no acceptable standard prescribing optimum
population size, and that although the pressures of population may
contribute to some social ills, they are not the primary cause of
them. Those who respond to the population problem in this way
point the finger in other causal directions to account for environmental decay—to our economic system, which encourages environmental destruction, to our technology which is responsible for
high-polluting individualized transportation, and to our minimal
emphasis on public or mass transit and so on. They also point to
the fact that some nutrition experts give us assurance that food resources exist which would permit the feeding of the world's population even if it doubled.[4]

The point is, this argument continues, that a number of voluntary
moves can be undertaken to mitigate whatever causal influences
population growth has on our social ills. We can produce more
food, redistribute people, provide meaningful jobs for women outside the home, provide family planning programs, contraceptive
information and services, early abortions, voluntary sterilization,
and so on. Anything short of government coercion. Anything short
of violating or overriding what is taken to be a fundamental moral

3. Aldous Huxley, *Brave New World Revisited* (New York: Harper,
1965), and Robert Heilbroner, *An Inquiry into the Human Prospect* (New
York: Norton, 1974).

4. See Jean Mayer, "Toward a Non-Malthusian Population Policy,"
Milbank Memorial Fund Quarterly 47 (1969): 340–53.

and constitutional right—the right to procreate and to have as many children as one wants.[5]

The above is a brief sketch of the pro and con positions on the use of coercive measures. Both those who argue for and against coercion appeal to the notions of "human well-being" and "optimum population size." These are notoriously difficult and vague concepts. When used in any premise in an argument on population control, they carry heavy weight and should be scrutinized closely. I will not offer that scrutiny here—and it may well be that these concepts, like other value concepts, cannot be pinned down for all time. But I want to define "optimum population level" (and hence human well-being) to include those conditions which permit the maximization of human welfare, human freedom, and distributive justice. Admittedly, this does not take us too far, for there is, in turn, wide disagreement over the meaning of these three value concepts. Does maximum human welfare require that average happiness be greater, or does it require the highest total amount of happiness? Are there not different and conflicting criteria of distributive justice? Which is to be adopted? And is it not possible that the value of maximizing human welfare—whether we are speaking of the average or the highest total—conflicts under some circumstances with the values of both distributive justice and freedom? Under what system of priorities does one resolve such conflicts? These are but some of the issues at stake in speaking of optimum population size.

We cannot even begin to resolve these issues here (some would say they are not resolvable), but fortunately we do not have to. Even allowing for differences in the definition of these value concepts and in the notion of optimum population level, there is enough agreement on what constitutes an optimum population level to have mutual grounds for discussion, and it is generally recognized that the current threat is dire indeed. In countries like India, Bangladesh, and Niger, there is practically no chance to maximize human welfare, freedom, and social justice unless stringent population controls are put into effect. Indeed, if conditions worsen in such coun-

5. As stated in a United Nations Document signed by thirty heads of state with the endorsement of Secretary General U Thant: "The opportunity to decide the number and spacing of children is a basic human right." *Declaration on Population: The World Leader's Statement*, Studies in Family Planning No. 26 (Jan., 1968): 1-3.

tries, conditions may well approach the scarcity discussed by David Hume in which the very notion of social justice loses its significance.

Differences of factual assessment

Let us return to the two poles of thought on the use of coercive measures. Each side sees the facts and the values at stake in different ways. It is important to see how the sides differ in assessing the issue. Proponents argue that depression of the death rate through progress in medicine, added to the failure of voluntary controls to halt the exponential population growth, will force coercive measures, however uninviting or unattractive coercion may be. In our finite world, zero population growth must be attained. The only question is whether this will come about as a result of death control through starvation, mass disease, civil disorder and warfare, or whether it will come about as a result of birth control. Surely, this argument continues, it is preferable to limit births, even at the cost of curtailing some traditional freedoms, than to permit an increase in death and suffering and a decrease in the quality of human life.

Now I cannot reject this kind of logic. Surely birth control is preferable to death control. However, there are severe dangers in state control of birth and population and in social enginering. *Brave New World* could easily be upon us. But, if voluntary control will not work and if only the natural disasters of death control are left, surely the rational move is restriction of freedom. Even hard-line opponents of coercive measures agree to this choice, as in this passage from Berman:

> If the figures are as gloomy as a person like Paul Ehrlich seems to think they are, if we honestly believe that disaster is going to follow a failure to arrest the alarmingly high rates of growth in certain underdeveloped countries, I, as a prudent population planner, would not only sanction infanticide, I would seriously consider sanctioning the taking of human life, all people over 65, for example. If we are faced with disaster, like Mr. Holmes in that lifeboat in the middle of the ocean, who, in order to save the remaining people, had to toss overboard some of the passengers, then we must take very firm action. That's what the prudent man would do. That's what Mr. Holmes did when he was in that lifeboat in the middle of the ocean.[6]

6. Donald J. Berman, "A Lawyer's View of the Population Problem," in Donald T. Fox, editor, *The Role of Law in Population Planning* (Dobbs

Clearly, then, the basic disagreement between at least some opponents of coercive ZPG policies and advocates is not so much value premises but factual premises—factual assessments of the probable consequences of natural biological processes and the efficacy of voluntary controls.

I am inclined to agree with the skeptical demographers and with Professor Garrett Hardin and Professor Paul Ehrlich on the facts.[7] The outlook is dire, especially in some underdeveloped countries, and controls other than purely voluntary ones may have to be initiated. One province in India is presently considering the practice of compulsory sterilization after the birth of the third child. Obviously, the solution to the problem will have to be context-dependent. The measures employed must vary according to the severity of the problem in different countries.

Surely, we should explore and utilize, far more than we have, all of the voluntary procedures first. They have not been given a thorough try. Also, if coercion is justified, governments should surely move from the least coercive to the more coercive. (Hardin correctly observes that there is a spectrum of coercion, ranging from tax incentives to incarceration).[8] One also must make sure that coercive measures—tax incentives, for example—accord with acceptable principles of distributive justice: that they not place inequitable burdens on the poor (forcing them through economic attractions to have no children at all), and that they not have punitive effects on the children of the poor and disadvantaged (by withholding welfare payments and so on).

Professor Kenneth Boulding has suggested a solution (how much is tongue-in-cheek, I do not know) which he recognizes many will find absurd because of the unwillingness of mankind to face up to the population problem—namely, a system of marketable licenses to have children. Persons would be issued licenses permitting them to have 2 or 2.2 children. They could sell or exchange portions or all of their certificates on the market. He recognizes that there are problems with this scheme—and so do I—but he does believe that

Ferry, N.Y.: Oceana Publications, 1972), p. 54. [These are papers of the 16th Hammerskjold Forum held in New York in February, 1971.]

7. Garrett Hardin, *Exporing New Ethics for Survival: The Voyage of the Spaceship Beagle* (New York: Penguin, 1973); Paul R. Ehrlich, *The Population Bomb* (New York: Ballantine, 1968).

8. Hardin, *Exploring New Ethics for Survival*, p. 199.

it "combines the minimum of social control necessary to the solution of this problem with a maximum of individual liberty and ethical choice."[9] The objective at least is the right target.

Value differences between advocates and opponents

We have been focusing on factual disagreements between proponents and opponents of ZPG. This last suggestion, in which procreation is seen as a licensable privilege, not as an inalienable right, points us to what may well be fundamental value differences between advocates and opponents of coercive ZPG. Opponents tend to view the right to procreate as an inalienable right, either moral or constitutional. Proponents tend to view procreation as an existing right but certainly not inalienable; in fact it is a right which, like other rights, can be justifiably proscribed, overridden, or qualified if the public interest so requires, just as property rights may be qualified or restricted in the public interest. Some proponents of coercive ZPG seem to hold a utilitarian theory of rights, in which rights are seen as rule-utilitarian devices designed to maximize human happiness. In this theory, rights are modifiable if human happiness, and the conditions of life instrumentally related to the attainment of that happiness require modification. Some opponents of coercive ZPG will not allow such modification. It is a story for another occasion, but even if a purely utilitarian theory of rights is inadequate—and I believe it is—the alteration of some rights when they conflict with other rights, or when they conflict with the public welfare or the public interest, is still justifiable. Even inalienable rights are not unrestricted, as Locke made abundantly clear.

If coercion is required, it should be "mutual coercion mutually agreed upon," as Garrett Hardin puts it.[10] There are instruments for effecting such coercion within nations, but there is no such instrument among nations; and it is obvious that some countries will or can do little to solve their own population problem internally. Still, no country or set of countries can justifiably ram its own population policy down the throats of other countries, however rational that policy and its underlying beliefs. The beliefs (which may fly in the face of rational population policies), the liberty of other persons, and the autonomy of other countries must be respected. This does

9. Kenneth Boulding, *The Meaning of the Twentieth Century* (New York: Harper, 1964), p. 135.

10. Hardin, *Exploring New Ethics for Survival.*

not mean that it is immoral or unreasonable for affluent countries, who are asked to aid non-affluent ones with population and hunger problems, to stipulate conditions for that aid. This is a kind of coercion, of course. But as long as those stipulations are based on the objective of helping that country find its own solutions to its own food and population problems and are not the sort of coercion in which food and development aid is exchanged for political allegiance, they are not unreasonable. Nonetheless, the sort of mutually agreed upon coercion required for a realistic solution to the population and hunger problem will require much stronger, more effective international organizations than we now have—an effective world federation of states. It seems to me that it can only be through such an organization that the values discussed above as constituting optimal population limits can be brought to fruition and the awful moral choices embedded in the doctrine of triage avoided.[11]

A balanced view for diverse value frameworks

What can we say in summary about ZPG and the use of coercion to obtain it? Our value commitments and the facts confronting human life permit, at this time, a strengthened effort at voluntary controls. This might well work in some countries. If such efforts, joined with other causative factors—like the changing role of women—are ineffective, then our value commitments and the facts justify coercive government moves, which should be initiated with the least coercive measures. Different measures would be appropriate for different countries, depending on their particular situations.

The value framework justifying coercive moves could be of several kinds. There are forceful utilitarian arguments, as indicated above, for those who find the utilitarian framework acceptable. For those who, like myself, find pure utilitarianism inadequate and who worry about simplistic value trade-offs between rights and liberties and welfare or consequential considerations, there are alternative value frameworks which yield forceful arguments in favor of coercive controls. A mixed model like that of W. D. Ross, which balances rights, duties, and consequential concerns, is a distinct possi-

---

11. For a discussion of the doctrine of triage, see Garrett Hardin, "Lifeboat Ethics: The Case Against Helping the Poor," *Psychology Today* 8 (1974): 38–43; and his "Living On a Lifeboat," *Bioscience* 25 (1974): 561–68. See also Ward Greene, "Triage," *New York Times Magazine*, Jan. 5, 1975, pp. 9–11, 44–45, 51.

bility (though there are difficulties with Ross's view.)[12] A lexically ordered model, like that of John Rawls, in which a trade-off involving liberty must always be for the sake of liberty, is an alternative framework.[13] A Rawlsian rationale for restricting the right to procreate would require showing that restriction is necessary to preserve other liberties. It seems to me that in many countries that case can be made.

We cannot discuss here these alternative value frameworks. But I would point out that, given the conditions in a number of countries, any of these frameworks would justify some coercive measures. I would add that technology alone will not solve the problem. IUDs may be distributed by the millions. Millions of condoms may be dropped by helicopter. It will not be adequate. Attitudes must be changed and, in the process, very hard ethical and political choices will have to be made. The process could begin with the modification of pronatalist values, norms, and incentives, values which motivate people to bear more and more children; we can also stress parental obligations for childbearing and child-care. And, if the extremes of death control are upon us, we must restrict the right to procreate itself.

ZERO ECONOMIC GROWTH

Let us turn, more briefly, to the issue of zero economic growth (ZEG) which has been pressed by some economists and ecologists in recent years. As with ZPG, the approach to ZEG hangs on the viewer's assessment of facts, value commitments, and value priorities. As with ZPG I want to try to clarify some of the values at stake.

Factual issues of economic growth

The factual issues bearing on economic growth are very complex,[14] and the value principles themselves are fuzzy and problematic. It is commonplace today, for example, to recognize that

12. William David Ross, *The Right and the Good* (Oxford: Clarendon Pr., 1930).

13. John Rawls, *A Theory of Justice* (Cambridge, Mass.: Harvard Univ. Pr., 1971).

14. See, for example the two recent reports to the Club of Rome: Dennis Meadows et al., *The Limits to Growth* (New York: New American Library, 1972), and M. Mesarovic and E. Pestel, *Mankind at the Turning Point* (New York: E. P. Dutton, 1974).

social welfare or human economic welfare is not measurable by a rise or fall in GNP.[15] The GNP explicitly excludes all valued goods and services which are not traded on the market; also, it aggregates the dollar value of all goods and services, including what some call negative production—the cost of cleaning up oil spills, for example. Hence, a rise in GNP could indicate several steps back in human welfare. But even if this is agreed, it leaves a wide range for disagreement on what constitutes human welfare or genuine economic growth or progress. These are normative concepts, and their open-textured nature is a notorious feature. Before we can discuss in any clear-cut way the pros and cons of economic growth—whether zero or merely controlled growth—we must have a reasonably clear definition of economic growth. And it is important that this concept not be defined in such a manner that the interesting and important questions are begged by the definition itself. We need a reasonably neutral concept of economic growth or progress. A Marxist, for example, may argue that a capitalistic concept of economic growth involves a "fetishism of commodities," that persons existing in market economies "know the price of everything but the value of nothing," all of which results in excessive materialism and alienation. Explicit assumptions about human nature and human needs and the role of an economic system in fulfilling those needs are here at stake; and all of these assumptions, of course, are highly contestable. To take this package of assumptions into a discussion of no-growth may beg certain basic issues, just as it would be to enter the discussion committed to identifying economic growth with a rise in the GNP.

I confess considerable sympathy for the critics of the "growth-mania" in our society. There does seem to me to be excessive emphasis on production and consumption. The result of that excess is damage both to the environment and to human beings, whose lives become captive to the productive system. Any spelling out of what is meant by "excess" or "damage" will ultimately depend on very controversial value premises. I have alluded to the Marxist premise already. Take one more example. If Plato is correct, human beings

15. For discussion, see W. T. Blackstone, "Ethics and Ecology," in *Philosophy and Environmental Crisis* (Athens: Univ. of Georgia Pr., 1974), pp. 16–42. [Editor's note: a complete bibliography of the writings of Blackstone has been prepared by Joe F. Jones, a graduate student at the University of Georgia. See *Social Theory and Practice* 5 (1979): 239–42.]

are damaged when their souls are turned upside down, with the appetites governing reason and will. This inversion is the condition of modern Western man, many claim. It is not merely environmental or ecological homeostasis which is upset by excessive growth and consumption, it is also the human psyche—human homeostasis—which is damaged.

I would like to avoid such controversial premises or assumptions in approaching the no-growth issue—at least up to a certain point—and look for common premises on the basis of which we might proceed. This might at least delay the bogging-down process, the state of value intractability that often emerges. Ultimately there is no escaping the controversial premises, and even the attempt to delay may not get us very far. But let us try.

The idea, then, is to formulate the growth—no-growth issue in a neutral way, so that one's assessment of facts and one's value commitments come into play in a clear straightforward way, rather than as disguised, surreptitious premises. A reasonably clear and neutral operational definition of economic growth has been suggested by Professor Mancur Olsen. Economic growth is "what the Department of Commerce and comparable institutions in other countries define it to be: if real (that is, price deflated) Net National Product per capita has gone up, there has been economic growth, and otherwise there hasn't." [16]

Given this concept of economic growth as a rise of real per capita income, we have to ask what are the advantages and disadvantages of zero growth; this requires that we appeal to our various value principles and value commitments, our assessments of factual matters of various types, and our perception of the relationship of those facts and values.

Value issues of the growth and no-growth approaches

Let us suppose, for the sake of argument, that we are all committed to the maximization of human happiness and welfare and distributive justice, both national and international. Our question would then amount to asking whether a zero-growth policy would maximize human happiness and contribute to distributive justice (nationally and internationally). Let us assume for the moment that

16. Mancur Olsen, "Introduction" to "The No-Growth Society," *Daedalus* 102, no. 4 (Fall, 1973), p. 5.

these values are both clear and mutually acceptable. (As already noted there are significantly different views of human happiness and different theories or criteria of distributive justice. But I want to ignore these complexities for the moment.)[17]

Let me focus on the human welfare utility considerations first. Would economic growth contribute to or detract from these objectives? I do not believe that this question can be meaningfully answered in a simplistic or general way. Growth of a certain kind in certain areas and a concomitant rise of real per capita income may contribute to these goals; growth in other areas, detract. The conclusion depends on highly context-dependent facts. If energy resources are threatened, should we build skyscrapers which consume enormous amounts of energy? Should we move in the direction of public transportation systems and away from automobiles? Considering the necessity of adequate transportation, the facts about energy availability are essential to answering these questions, just as the facts about other areas—the effects of oil spillage in off-shore drilling—must be taken into consideration in those contexts. Different problems require different solutions. A generalized response—growth or no-growth—is simply inadequate.

17. I will also avoid for the moment the issue of whether there are values, intrinsic and instrumental, other than those associated with humans (values of nature) which ought to be preserved in their own right and which ought to play a key role in growth decisions. Some (see, for example, C. Stone, "Should Trees Have Standing? Toward Legal Rights for Natural Objects," *Southern California Law Review* 45 (1972): 450–501) would argue that there are such values, and further that natural entities and processes like trees and rivers have rights along with animals, and that those values and rights —even if they were not instrumentally related to human welfare, which they are—must be included in a framework of decision-making on economic growth.

Basic issues in theory of value and theory of rights are raised by such claims. Here it might simply be observed that a theory of value like that of Ralph Barton Perry [*Realms of Value*, (Cambridge, Mass.: Harvard Univ. Pr., 1954)] in which value is defined in terms of "any object of any interest" might move one well beyond the anthropocentric view of value with which many operate and which is so decried by many environmentalists; but I am sceptical about the conceptual propriety of ascribing rights to rocks, trees, and rivers themselves. (For discussion of conceptual requirements for ascription of rights, see Joel Feinberg, "The Rights of Animals and Unborn Generations," pp. 43–68, in W. T. Blackstone, ed., *Philosophy and Environmental Crisis*, and his "The Nature and Value of Rights," *The Journal of Value Inquiry* 4 (1970): 263–67.

One can hardly dispute the logical point that exponential economic growth cannot continue forever in a world of finite resources. Moreover, there are some general facts about the effects of uncontrolled economic growth which can be ignored only at the peril of mankind. If ecologists are correct, the capacity of the ecosystem to absorb waste is limited, and uncontrolled growth is a threat to the natural life support systems on which human existence and other forms of life depend. The capacity of the environment to perform the essential functions of nutrient cycling, climate regulation, and pest control is threatened by some types of growth. Non-renewable, non-reproducible natural resources are rapidly being exhausted. The ecologist-environmentalist is forcing us to an awareness of these facts. It may be that in the long run—how long I cannot say—these threatening conditions will require, for utilitarian-survival reasons, the adopting of a no-growth economy. But a straightforward no-growth response to these facts at the present time is inadequate. Surely growth decisions should be based on specific facts and projections about the impact of growth. Some growth may be linked with high rates of pollution, depletion of resources, negative esthetic impact, and so on. Other growth may not be so linked, especially growth in the area of human services. Roland McKean wisely states "holding GNP or any other practicable index of input constant to reduce pollution or the consumption of stored-up energy is like holding a a consumer's total budget constant in order to reduce his disposal of trash along the highway or his consumption of fats." [18]

Furthermore, a strict no-growth policy would require imposing ceilings on all industries, and this in turn would require a centrally planned and controlled economy—far more centrally controlled than the system now operative in this country. In fact, strict no-growth would require effective international controls. The effects of such a shift in economic and political systems must also be taken into consideration in opting for a no-growth policy. Many would maintain that the threat to human existence would have to be great indeed to justify this shift.

Of course, a no-growth policy is one thing. But increasing controls on economic growth and activity is another matter. There are social and political implications of such controls, though not nearly

18. Roland McKean, "Growth vs. No-Growth: An Evaluation," *Daedalus* 102, no. 4 (Fall, 1973), p. 219.

as severe as no-growth. Agencies like the Environmental Protection Agency come into being; individuals and groups are restricted from certain actions by the arm of the law. Surely, though, the facts and our value commitments justify some of these restrictions. Gene Odum speaks of "preventive legislation," and E. J. Mishan speaks of laws which shift the burden of proof and the cost of redress for environmental degradation from the general public to the industries which produce it.[19] Is the social benefit worth the cost in terms of freedom and higher prices? Yes, if I understand the ecological facts correctly. Indeed the facts justify other forms of legal and social coercion to control growth: subsidies on land, taxes, and zoning laws can be used to help assure appropriate land-use in specific contexts without blocking economic growth.

What I am suggesting is a context-dependent calculation of effects or probable effects of economic growth on human (and animal) well-being. And since the effects of growth have different impacts on different individuals, groups, and institutions, the calculation must include these different effects. For example, mobility of persons generally accompanies economic growth, and many concerned with the stability of the family insist that the negative impact of growth on family life weighs against a growth policy. Others hold that the stability of the traditional family is less important than the economic justice facilitated by a growth policy. Surely both of these values are important and should be weighed. In fact, nearly an infinity of possible consequences of a zero-growth policy must be considered in the calculations—the impact on scientific research and in turn the impact of that change on health, education and welfare; the impact on undeveloped nations, on future generations, on esthetic, cultural, and recreational conditions of human life, and so on. No exact calculation is possible. This does not mean, however, that we should throw up our hands and do nothing. We should heed Aristotle's admonition in the *Nicomachean Ethics* to expect only the degree of certainty which the subject matter permits, and

19. Eugene Odum, "Preventive Law" in *Life* (*Legal Information for Environmentalists*, a publication of the Environmental Law Society of the University of Georgia School of Law), vol. I, no. I (1975): 4. See also Eugene Odum, "Environmental Ethic and the Attitude Revolution," pp. 10–15, in W. T. Blackstone, ed., *Philosophy and Environmental Crisis*. Also, see E. J. Mishan, "Ills, Bads, and Disamenities: The Wages of Growth," *Daedalus* 102, no. 4 (Fall, 1973), p. 83.

then seek it. Recognition of this uncertainty and my emphasis on a context-dependent assessment of the impact of growth should in no way be construed as a rejection of the ecological attitude and concern for environmental impact.[20] On the contrary, this emphasis facilitates the recognition that far too much economic growth, including that in forestry and agriculture, is linked to environmental degradation. Such growth may provide temporary benefits, but in the long run it contributes to poverty by impairing the life-support capacity of the land. The editors of *Ceres*, a United Nations magazine, point out that "it is no coincidence that the forests of all the countries with major crop failures in recent years due to drought or floods—Bangladesh, Ethiopia, India, Pakistan, and the Sahel countries—had been razed to the ground."[21] Efforts to increase production cannot ignore fundamental ecological facts. Recognition of such facts and their relationship to long-range human wellbeing (and it must be admitted that gathering the facts on ecological deterioration is a difficult and slow task) does not require a policy of zero economic growth. In fact such a policy would in all likelihood conflict with this objective. What is required by ecological and utilitarian considerations is a policy of controlled growth with sensitivity to highly context-dependent facts.

Let me now turn to the other value principle mentioned as important in assessing the emphasis on the zero economic growth, namely, distributive justice. Most of what I have said so far fits a cost-benefit or utilitarian framework of analysis of the no-growth issue. But any evaluation of no-growth must also consider the implications of such a policy for the goal of distributive justice, both national and international.[22] We have done little enough to effect distributive justice in a growth economy. But if Lester Thurow is correct, under a zero-growth economy "the distribution of family income would gradually grow more unequal, blacks would fall further behind whites, and the share going to female earnings would fall below what it would

20. For discussion, see W. T. Blackstone, "Ethics and Ecology," *Philosophy and Environmental Crisis.*

21. András Biró, "The Nurturing Forest," *Ceres* 8 (Mar./Apr., 1975; No. 2): 4.

22. I am assuming, without here treating any of the philosophical issues at stake, that it makes sense to speak of distributive justice among nations; also, that justice and utility are not reducible to one another.

otherwise be."[23] I am inclined to agree with this conclusion. Under zero growth there is less to distribute, whatever the criteria of distribution; also what one person gains, someone else loses. By contrast, in a growth economy gains are possible for the young, for minorities, and for women, without someone or some other class losing or being set back.

Suppose, for example, we were operating with John Rawls's theory of distributive justice (which is, of course, quite controversial) and applying it under no-growth conditions, assuming for the moment that it is applicable under those conditions.[24] The "difference principle" in his theory requires that all inequalities in the distribution of goods and services be justified, and justification requires showing that those inequalities contribute to an increase in the standard of living of those at the bottom of the economic ladder. (The principle of equal liberty and that of fair equal opportunity do have lexical priority over the difference principle, and, in a detailed analysis, the consequences of that priority must be spelled out.) Even without a ceiling on growth and on the pool of resources available for distribution, the burden of proof imposed by the difference principle would probably result in some taking away from the rich and giving to the poor; a no-growth economy would require even greater redistribution. I am not arguing against redistribution. I am simply pointing out that the pains of redistribution will be much greater under a no-growth economy. Some of those pains must be faced even under a less extreme, controlled growth economy (as the *Defunis* case plainly shows[25]).

A similar sort of problem would exist if zero-growth policy were internationalized. I cannot imagine underdeveloped countries— nor, indeed, developed countries—agreeing to such a policy. But if they did, it would probably make the proportionate differences in living standards between the developed and undeveloped nations

23. See Lester Thurow, "The Impact of Zero Economic Growth on Personal Incomes," Mimeo., M.I.T., August, 1972, quoted by Richard Zeckhauser, "The Risks of Growth," *Daedalus* 102, no. 4 (Fall, 1973), p. 109.

24. John Rawls, *A Theory of Justice*.

25. *Defunis v. Odegaard* 94 S. Ct. 1704 (1974). [Editor's note: for Blackstone's views of this Defunis case, see his article "Reverse Discrimination and Compensatory Justice," *Social Theory and Practice* 3 (Spring, 1975): 253–88.]

even greater; concomitantly, conflicts of interest would increase greatly between undeveloped countries and countries like the United States, where 6 percent of the world's population consumes about 40 percent of the world's energy and products. Those conflicts are acute enough as it is. Very little has been done by rich, industrialized countries to lessen the gross differences in standards of living between themselves and undeveloped countries. Less than 1 percent of the U.S. budget goes for foreign aid. The same is true of most other developed countries. Even controlled growth, as contrasted to zero growth, will exacerbate these differences.

I do not by any means wish to imply that economic growth will produce human equality or necessarily bring economic improvement to the poor. Redistribution will be required in any case. But economic growth makes redistribution much easier. The emphasis on ecological-environmental data and the restrictions they mandate simply adds to the imperative nature of this distribution, for it makes it plain that we cannot sit back and hope that exponential growth will painlessly solve the problem for us.

Economic growth would make distributive justice easier to attain. But does distributive justice actually require economic growth? Great progress would be made toward the goal of distributive justice without any economic growth. If certain fundamental changes were made in the basis on which goods and services are distributed, and if the attitude which equates greater well-being with greater levels of consumption were altered, considerable progress could be made within current production levels. But given the magnitude of need of undeveloped countries, the existence of hundreds of millions of malnourished and starving persons world-wide, I believe that a flat-out zero-growth policy would effectively preclude the distribution required to solve this problem. In this sense, distributive justice requires what Howard Richards calls "productive justice,"[26]

26. See Howard Richards' "Productive Justice," a paper presented at the American Philosophical Association, Eastern Division, New York, New York, Dec. 26–29, 1974. Richards offers several arguments for considering production to be an obligation of justice. One is this: if a minimum level below which no one should fall is a requirement of distributive justice, and if that minimum level cannot be achieved without production, then production is a requirement or obligation of justice. The problem is establishing this first premise, but if it holds, then malnourished and starving persons have a right,

the production of the maximal levels of goods required to fulfill basic needs consistent with the avoidance of ecological catastrophe.

Our analysis of the zero economic growth question within a utilitarian framework indicated that that framework does not require or support a blanket zero-growth policy; so too, the appeal to distributive justice by no means requires and may be incompatible with a zero-growth emphasis. One makes this claim with trepidation, given the enormity and complexity of extending and applying the principle of distributive justice to generations yet unborn, as both prominent utilitarians and non-utilitarians (such as Rawls) alike would have us do. Of course, I do not mean that economic growth should not be controlled, nor that our current values and attitudes concerning growth and standards of consumption should remain intact. E. F. Schumacher may be correct. In *Small is Beautiful*, he argues that greater consumption does not necessarily mean greater well-being and that we can meet our needs better by scaling down our wants (which are often artificial) and by shooting for maximum well-being with minimum consumption.[27] I think that nothing I have said is incompatible with the major thrust of his position. Even a "Buddhist economics" (the title of a key chapter in Schumacher's book) would seem to require some growth to fulfill genuine human needs. The controlled growth favored in this essay, stressing a context-dependent assessment, is also consistent with the current emphasis on economic models quite different from the Western one (which emphasizes large scale organization, highly centralized planning, mass production, heavy capital investment, and highly advanced technology). These alternative economic models might be better for non-Western countries. In fact, they might be better for much of the West.

---

if not to food itself, at least to the highest level of food production consistent with the avoidance of ecological catastrophe (which would in fact assure the existence of adequate food for all).

27. E. F. Schumacher, *Small Is Beautiful: Economics as if People Mattered* (New York: Harper, 1975), p. 57.

III

Racism, Sexism, and Preferential Treatment
An Approach to the Topics[1]
Richard Wasserstrom

RACISM AND SEXISM ARE UNDENIABLY central topics to most Americans; but, while there is relatively little disagreement about their importance as topics, there is substantial, vehement, and apparently intractable disagreement about what individuals, practices, ideas, and institutions are either racist or sexist—and for what reasons. The disputed questions concern how individuals and institutions ought to regard and respond to matters relating to race or sex.

One example concerns those programs of "affirmative action," "preferential treatment," or "reverse discrimination" that are a feature of much of our institutional life. Attitudes and beliefs about these programs are diverse. Some people—a majority, I suspect—are sorely troubled by these programs. They are convinced that some features of some programs, such as quotas, are indefensible and wrong. Other features and programs are tolerated, but not with fervor or enthusiasm. Another group with a very different view thinks these programs are important and appropriate. They do not see these programs, quotas included, as racist or sexist, but they see much about the dominant societal institutions that is. They regard the racism and sexism of the society as accounting substantially for the failure or refusal to adopt such programs willingly and to press vigorously for their full implementation.

Much of the confusion in thinking and arguing about racism, sexism, and affirmative action results from a failure to see that there

1. [Editor's note: This paper was published in a more comprehensive form in the *U.C.L.A. Law Review* 24 (1977): 581–622; a revised and expanded treatment of these ideas can be found in *Philosophy and Social Issues: Five Studies* (Notre Dame, Ind.: Univ. of Notre Dame Pr., 1980).]

are three different perspectives within which the topics of racism, sexism, and affirmative action can most usefully be examined. The first of these perspectives concentrates on what in fact is true of the culture, on the social realities. Here the fundamental question concerns the culture itself: what are its institutions, attitudes and ideologies in respect to matters of race and sex?

The second perspective is concerned with the way things ought to be. From this perspective, analysis focuses very largely on possible, desirable states of affairs. Here the fundamental question concerns ideals: what would the good society—in terms of its institutions, its attitudes, and its values—look like in respect to matters involving race and sex?

The third perspective looks forward to the means by which the ideal may be achieved. Its focus is on the question: what is the best or most appropriate way to move from the existing social realities, whatever they happen to be, to a closer approximation of the ideal society? This perspective is concerned with instrumentalities.

Many of the debates over affirmative action and over what things are racist and sexist are unilluminating because they neglect to take into account these three perspectives, all of which are important and each of which must be considered separately. While I do not claim that all the significant normative and conceptual questions concerning race, sex, or affirmative action can be made to disappear, I do believe that an awareness and use of these perspectives can produce valuable insights that contribute to their resolution. In particular, the question of whether something is racist or sexist is not as straightforward or unambiguous as may appear at first. For the question may be about social realities, about how the categories of race or sex function in the culture and to what effect. Or the question may be about ideals, about what the good society would make of race or sex. Or the question may be about instrumentalities: about how, given the social realities as to race and sex, to achieve a closer approximation of the ideal. Therefore, what might be an impermissible way to take race into account in the ideal society, may also be a desirable or perfectly appropriate way to take race into account given the social realities.

It is these three different perspectives and these underlying issues that I am interested in exploring. I use this framework to clarify a number of the central matters that are involved in thinking clearly about the topics of racism, sexism and affirmative action. Within this framework I explore some of the analogies and disanalogies between racism and sexism—some of the ways they are analytically interchangeable phenomena and some of the ways they are not. And I examine some of the key arguments that most often arise whenever these topics are considered. In respect to programs of affirmative action, or preferential treatment, I argue specifically that much of the opposition to such programs is not justifiable. It rests upon confusion in thinking about the relevant issues and upon a failure to perceive and appreciate some of the ways in which our society is racist and sexist. I argue that there is much to be said for the view that such programs (even when they include quotas) are defensible and right.

SOCIAL REALITIES

One way to think and talk about racism and sexism is to concentrate upon the perspective of the social realities. Here one must begin by insisting that to talk about either is to talk about a particular social and cultural context. In our own culture the first thing to observe is that race and sex are socially important categories. They are so in virtue of the fact that we live in a culture which has, throughout its existence, made race and sex extremely important characteristics of and for all the people living in the culture.

It is surely possible to imagine a culture in which race would be an unimportant, insignificant characteristic of individuals. In such a culture race would be largely if not exclusively a matter of superficial physiology; a matter, we might say, simply of the way one looked. If it were, any analysis of race and racism would necessarily assume very different dimensions from what they do in our society. In such a culture, the meaning of the term "race" would itself have to change substantially: in such a culture it would literally make no sense to say of a person that he or she was "passing." This can be said and understood in our own culture and it shows at least that to talk of race is to talk of more than the way one looks.

Sometimes, when people talk about what is wrong with affirmative action programs, or programs of preferential hiring, they say that what is wrong with such programs is that they take a thing as superficial as an individual's race and turn it into something important. They say that a person's race does not matter; other things do, such as qualifications. Whatever else may be said of such statements, as descriptions of the social realities they seem to be simply false. One fact about our society is that the race of an individual is much more than a matter of superficial physiology. It is, instead, one of the dominant characteristics that affects both the way the individual looks at the world and the way the world looks at the individual. As I have said, that need not be the case. It may in fact be very important that we work toward a society in which that would not be the case, but it is the case now and it must be understood in any adequate and complete discussion of racism. That is why, too, it does not make much sense when people sometimes say that they would treat a green Martian the same way they treat people exactly like themselves. Part of our social and cultural history is to treat people of certain races in a certain way, and we do not have a social or cultural history of treating green people from Mars in any particular way. To put it simply, the social realities of race and racism are not simply questions of how some people respond to people whose skins are of different hues, irrespective of the social context.

I can put the point still another way: our culture does not treat eye color as it does race. Eye color is an irrelevant category; nobody cares what color people's eyes are; it is not an important cultural fact; nothing turns on what eye color you have. It is important to see that race is not like that at all. In our culture, to be nonwhite—and especially to be black—is to be treated and viewed as a member of a group different from and inferior to the group of standard, fully developed persons, the adult white males. To be black is to be a member of what was a despised minority and what is still a disliked and oppressed one. That is simply part of the awful truth of our cultural and social history, and a significant feature of the social reality of our culture today.

It is even clearer that one's sexual identity is a centrally important, crucially relevant category within our culture. I think, in fact, that it is more important and more fundamental than one's race. Obviously, there are substantially different role expectations and role assignments to persons in accordance with their sexual physiology, and the positions of the two sexes in the culture are distinct. We do have a patriarchal society in which it matters enormously whether one is a male or a female. By almost all important measures it is more advantageous to be a male rather than a female.

Women and men are socialized differently. We learn very early and forcefully that we are either males or females and that much turns upon which sex one is. The evidence seems overwhelming and well-documented that sex roles play a fundamental role in the way persons think of themselves and the world—to say nothing of the way the world thinks of them. Men and women are taught to see men as independent, capable, and powerful, and to see women as dependent, limited in abilities, and passive. A woman's success or failure in life is defined largely in terms of her activities within the family, and her status in society is determined in substantial measure by the vocation and success of her husband. Economically, women are much worse off than men. They receive no pay for work done in the home. As members of the labor force their wages are significantly lower than those paid to men, even when they are engaged in similar work and have similar educational backgrounds. The higher the prestige or the salary of the job, the fewer women in the labor force. And, of course, women are conspicuously absent from most positions of authority and power in the major economic and political institutions of our society.

We can see fairly easily that the sexual categories, like the racial ones, are in important respects products of the society. Like one's race, one's sex is not merely or even primarily a matter of physiology. To see this we need only realize that we can understand the idea of a transsexual. A transsexual is someone who would describe himself or herself either as a person who is essentially a female but through some accident of nature is trapped in a male body, or vice versa. His (or her) description is a short-hand way of saying that he (or she) is more comfortable with the role allocated by the culture to people who are physiologically of the opposite sex. That we regard this assertion of the transsexual as intelligible shows how deep the notion of sexual identity is in our culture and how little it has to do with physiology. Because we can understand what passing and transsexuality mean, we can see that the existing social categories of both race and sex are in this sense creations of the culture.

Again, as is true for race, it is also a significant social fact that to be a female is to be viewed as different from the standard, fully developed person, who is male as well as white. But to be female, as opposed to being black, is not to be conceived of as simply a creature of less worth. This fact differentiates sexism from racism: the ideology of sex, as opposed to the ideology of race, is a good deal more complex and confusing. Women are both put on a pedestal and deemed not fully developed persons. They are idealized; their approval and admiration is sought; and they are at the same time regarded as less competent than men and less able to live fully developed, fully human lives—for that is what men do. Because the sexual ideology is complex, confusing, and variable, it does not unambiguously proclaim the female to be of lesser value than the male, nor does it unambiguously correspond to the existing social realities. For these and other reasons, sexism can plausibly be regarded as a deeper phenomenon than racism, more deeply embedded in the culture and hence less visible. Harder to detect, it is harder to eradicate. Moreover, it is less unequivocally regarded as unjust and unjustifiable. That is, there is less agreement within the dominant ideology that sexism even implies an unjustifiable practice or attitude. Hence, many persons announce, without regret or embarrassment, that they are sexists or male chauvinists; very few announce openly that they are racists. For all of these reasons sexism may be a more insidious evil than racism, but there is little merit in trying to decide between two seriously objectionable practices which one is worse.

While I do not think that I have made very controversial claims about either our cultural history or our present-day culture, I am aware that my claims have been stated very imprecisely and that I have offered little evidence to substantiate them. If we were to reflect seriously upon our culture, we should be able, in a crude way, both to understand and to agree with these claims. But I imagine that an accurate description of the social realities of race and sex can be derived only from a thorough description of our society— our institutions, practices, attitudes, and ideology. Such a description would require not only the cooperation of the social sciences, but also that they be value-free and unaffected by the fact that most of their practitioners are white males.

Viewed from the perspective of social reality, it should be clear, too, that racism and sexism should not be thought of as simply taking a person's race or sex into account, or even simply taking a person's race or sex into account in an arbitrary way. Instead— and I think this is important—racism and sexism consist in taking race and sex into account in a certain way in the context of a specific set of institutional arrangements and a specific ideology which together create and maintain a *system* of unjust institutions and unwarranted beliefs and attitudes. In this system, political, economic, and social power is concentrated in the hands of white males.

One way to understand this system is to consider segregated bathrooms. We know, for instance, that it is wrong, clearly racist, to
have racially segregated bathrooms. How, then, are we to account
for them? The answer is to be found through a consideration of
the role that the practice of racially segregated bathrooms played
in that system of racial segregation we had in the United States—
through, in other words, an examination of the social realities.
Racially segregated bathrooms were an important part of that
system, the ideology of which was complex and perhaps not even
internally consistent. A significant feature of the ideology was that
blacks were not only less than fully developed humans, but that
they were also dirty and impure. They were the sorts of creatures
who could and would contaminate white persons if they came into
certain kinds of contact with them—in the bathroom, at the dinner
table, or in bed, although it was appropriate for blacks to prepare
and handle food, and even to nurse white babies. This ideology
was intimately related to a set of institutional arrangements and
power relationships in which whites were politically, economically,
and socially dominant. The ideology supported the institutional arrangements, and the institutional arrangements reinforced the ideology. The net effect was that racially segregated bathrooms were
both a part of the institutional mechanism of oppression and an
instantiation of this ideology of racial taint. The point of maintaining racially segregated bathrooms was not in any simple or
direct sense to keep both whites and blacks from using each other's
bathrooms; it was to make sure that blacks would not contaminate
bathrooms used by whites. The practice also taught both whites
and blacks that certain kinds of contacts were forbidden because
whites would be degraded by the contact with the blacks.

The failure to understand the character of these institutions of
racial oppression is what makes some of the judicial reasoning
about racial discrimination against blacks so confusing and unsatis-
factory. At times when the courts have tried to explain what is con-
stitutionally wrong with racial segregation, they have said that the
problem is that race is an inherently suspect category. What they
have meant by this, or been thought to mean by this, is that any
differentiation among human beings on the basis of racial identity
is inherently unjust, because arbitrary, and therefore any particular
case of racial differentiation must be shown to be fully rational and
justifiable. But the primary evil of the various schemes of racial

segregation against blacks that the courts were being called upon to assess was not that they were a capricious and irrational way of allocating public benefits and burdens. That might well be the primary wrong with racial segregation if we lived in a society very different from the one we have. The primary evil of these schemes was instead that they designedly and effectively marked all black persons as degraded, dirty, less than fully developed persons who were unfit for full membership in the political, social, and moral community.

It is worth observing both that there is no common conception that it is wrong to have sexually segregated bathrooms and that the social reality of sexually segregated bathrooms appears to be different. The idea behind such sexual segregation seems to be essentially concerned with the mutual undesirability of the use by both sexes of the same bathroom at the same time. There is no notion of the possibility of contamination, or even directly of inferiority and superiority. What seems to be involved—at least in part—is the importance of inculcating and preserving a sense of secrecy concerning the genitalia of the opposite sex. What seems to be at stake is the maintenance of that same sense of mystery or forbiddenness about the sexuality of the other sex which is fostered by the general prohibition upon public nudity and the unashamed viewing of genitalia.

Sexually segregated bathrooms simply play a different role in our culture than did racially segregated ones. But that is not to say that the role they play is either benign or unobjectionable—only that it is different. Sexually segregated bathrooms may well be objectionable, but, here too, not on the ground that they are prima facie capricious or arbitrary. Rather, the case against them now would rest on the ground that they are, perhaps, one small part of that scheme of sex-role differentiation which uses the mystery of sexual anatomy, among other things, to maintain the primacy of heterosexual attraction central to our version of the patriarchal system of power relationships. Whether sexually segregated bathrooms would be objectionable, because irrational, in the good society depends upon what the good society would look like in respect to sexual differentiation.

IDEALS

We now come to the second perspective, described at the outset, which is also important for understanding and analyzing racism and sexism. It is the perspective of the ideal. Just as we can and must ask what is involved today in our culture in being of one race or of one sex rather than the other, and how individuals are in fact viewed and treated, we can also ask different questions: namely, what would the good or just society make of race and sex, and to what degree, if at all, would racial and sexual distinctions ever be taken into account? Indeed, it could plausibly be argued that we could not have an adequate idea of whether a society was racist or sexist unless we had some conception of what a thoroughly non-racist or nonsexist society would look like. This perspective is ex-tremely instructive and often neglected. Comparatively little theo-retical literature dealing with either racism or sexism has concerned itself in a systematic way with this perspective.

In order to consider more precisely some of the possible ideals of desirable racial or sexual differentiation, we must first ask: "In respect to what?" One way to do this is to distinguish among three levels or areas of social and political arrangements and activities. First, there is the area of basic political rights and obligations, in-cluding the rights to vote and to travel, and the obligation to pay in-come taxes. Second, there is the area of important nongovernmental institutional benefits and burdens. Examples are access to and em-ployment in significant economic markets, the opportunity to ac-quire and enjoy housing in the setting of one's choice, the right of persons who want to marry each other to do so, and the duties (nonlegal as well as legal) that persons acquire in getting married. And third, there is the area of individual, social interaction, includ-ing such matters as whom one will have as friends, and what esthetic preferences one will cultivate and enjoy.

For each of these three areas we can ask, for example, whether in a nonracist society it would be thought appropriate ever to take the race of the individuals into account. Thus, one picture of a non-racist society is that which is captured by what I call the assimila-tionist ideal: a nonracist society would be one in which the race of an individual would be the functional equivalent of eye color in our society. In our society no basic political rights and obligations are determined on the basis of eye color. No important institutional benefits and burdens are connected with eye color. Indeed, except for the mildest sort of esthetic preferences, a person would be thought odd who made even private, social decisions by taking eye color into account. And for reasons that we could readily state we could explain why it would be wrong to permit anything but the mildest, most trivial esthetic preference to turn on eye color. The reasons would concern the irrelevance of eye color for any political or social institution, practice, or arrangement. According to the assimilationist ideal, in a nonracist society an individual's race would be of no more significance in any of these three areas than is eye color today.

The assimilationist ideal in respect to sex does not seem to be as readily plausible and obviously attractive here as it is in the case of race. In fact, many persons invoke the possible realization of the assimilationist ideal as a reason for rejecting the Equal Rights Amendment and indeed the idea of women's liberation itself. My own view is that the assimilationist ideal may be just as good and just as important an ideal in respect to sex as it is in respect to race. But many persons think there are good reasons why an assimilationist society in respect to sex would not be desirable.

To be sure, to make the assimilationist ideal a reality in respect to sex would involve more profound and fundamental revisions of our institutions and our attitudes than would be the case in respect to race. On the institutional level we would have to alter radically our practices concerning the family and marriage. If a nonsexist society is a society in which one's sex is no more significant than eye color in our society today, then laws which require the persons who are getting married to be of different sexes would clearly be sexist laws.

On the level of attitude and idea, the assimilationist ideal would require the eradication of all sex-role differentiation. It would never teach about the inevitable or essential attributes of masculinity or femininity; it would never encourage or discourage the ideas of sisterhood or brotherhood; and it would be unintelligible to talk about the virtues as well as disabilities of being a woman or a man. Were sex like eye color, these things would make no sense. Just as the normal, typical adult is virtually oblivious to the eye color of other persons for all major interpersonal relationships, so the normal, typical adult in this kind of nonsexist society would be indifferent to the sexual, physiological differences of other persons for all interpersonal relationships.

To acknowledge that things would be very different is, of course, hardly to concede that they would be undesirable. But still, perhaps the problem is with the assimilationist ideal. And the assimilationist ideal is certainly not the only possible, plausible ideal.

There are, for instance, two others that are closely related, but distinguishable. One I call the ideal of diversity; the other, the ideal of tolerance. Both can be understood by considering how religion, rather than eye color, is thought about in our culture. According to the ideal of diversity, heterodoxy in respect to religious belief and practice is regarded as a positive good. In this view there would be a loss—it would be a worse society—were everyone to be a member of the same religion. According to the other view, the ideal of tolerance, heterodoxy in respect to religious belief and practice would be seen more as a necessary, lesser evil. In this view there is nothing intrinsically better about diversity in respect to religion, but the evils of achieving anything like homogeneity far outweigh the possible benefits.

Whatever differences there might be between the ideals of diversity and tolerance, the similarities are more striking. Under neither ideal would it be thought that the allocation of basic political rights and duties should take an individual's religion into account. And we would want equalitarianism even in respect to most important institutional benefits and burdens—for example, access to employment in desirable vocations. Nonetheless, in both views it would be deemed appropriate to have some institutions (typically those which are connected in an intimate way with these religions) which take the religion of members of the society into account. For example, it might be thought permissible and appropriate for members of a religious group to join together in collective associations which have religious, educational and social dimensions. And on the individual, interpersonal level, it might be thought unobjectionable, or in the diversity view, even admirable, were persons to select their associates, friends, and mates on the basis of their religious orientation. So there are two possible and plausible ideals of what the good society would look like in respect to religion: one in which religious differences would be to some degree maintained because the diversity of religions would be seen either as an admirable, valuable feature of the society, or a second in which such diversity would be tolerated. The picture is more complex and less easily described than that of the assimilationist ideal.

It may be that in respect to sex (and conceivably even in respect to race) something more like one of these ideals is the right one. But one problem then—and a very substantial one—is to specify with a good deal of precision and care what that ideal really comes to. Which legal, institutional, and personal differentiations are permissible and which are not? Which attitudes and beliefs concerning sexual identification and difference are properly introduced and maintained and which are not? Part, but by no means all, of the attractiveness of the assimilationist ideal is its clarity and simplicity. In the good society of the assimilationist sort we would be able to tell easily and unequivocally whether any law, practice or attitude was in any respect either racist or sexist. Part, but by no means all, of the unattractiveness of any pluralistic ideal is that it makes the question of what is racist or sexist much more difficult and complicated. But although simplicity and lack of ambiguity may be virtues, they are not the only virtues to be taken into account in deciding among competing ideals. We quite appropriately take other considerations to be relevant to an assessment of the value and worth of alternative nonracist and nonsexist societies.

I do not mean to suggest even that all persons who reject the assimilationist ideal in respect to sex would necessarily embrace either something like the ideal of tolerance or the ideal of diversity. Some persons might think the right ideal is one in which substantially greater sexual differentiation and sex-role identification is retained than would be the case under either of these conceptions. Thus, someone might believe that the good society would be, perhaps, essentially like the one they think we now have in respect to sex: one with equality of political rights, such as the right to vote, but with all of the sexual differentiation in both legal and nonlegal institutions that is characteristic of our society. And someone might also believe that the usual ideological justifications for these arrangements are correct and appropriate.

This could, of course, be regarded as a version of the ideal of diversity, with the emphasis upon the extensive character of the institutional and personal difference connected with sexual identity. Whether it is a kind of ideal of diversity or a different ideal altogether turns, I think, upon two things: first, how pervasive the sexual differentiation is; second, whether the ideal contains a conception of the appropriateness of significant institutional and interpersonal inequality—for example, that the woman's job is, in large measure, to serve and be dominated by the male. The more this latter feature is present, the clearer the case for regarding this as an ideal distinct from any of those described so far.

The next question, of course, is how to make a rational choice among these different, possible ideals. One place to begin is with the empirical world. For the question of whether an ideal is plausible and attractive turns in part on the nature of the empirical world. If it is true, for example, that race is not only a socially significant category in our culture but that it is largely a socially created one as well, then many ostensible objections to the assimilationist ideal immediately disappear. It is obvious that we could formulate and use some sort of a crude, incredibly imprecise physiological concept of race. In this sense we could even say that race is a naturally occurring rather than a socially created feature of the world. Diverse skin colors and related physiological characteristics are distributed among human beings. But the fact is that except for skin hue and related physiological characteristics, race is a socially created category. And it is essential to see that race as a naturally occurring characteristic is a socially irrelevant category. There do not, in fact, appear to be any characteristics that are part of this natural concept * of race that are in any plausible way even prima facie relevant to the appropriate distribution of political, institutional, or interpersonal concerns in the good society. Because, in this sense, race is like eye color, there is no plausible case to be made on this ground against the assimilationist ideal.

There is, of course, the social reality of race. In creating and tolerating a society in which race matters, we must recognize that we have created a vastly more complex concept of race which includes what might be called the idea of ethnicity as well—a set of attitudes, traditions, beliefs, and the like, which the society has made part of what it means to be of a race. It may be, therefore, that one could argue that a form of the pluralist ideal ought to be preserved in respect to race (in the socially created sense), for reasons similar to those that might be offered in support of the desirability of some version of the pluralist ideal in respect to religion. As I have indicated, I am skeptical, but for the purposes of this essay it can well be left an open question.

Despite appearances, the case of sex is more like that of race than is often thought. What opponents of assimilationism seize upon is that sexual difference appears to be a naturally occurring category of obvious and inevitable social relevance in a way or to a degree that race is not. There are two problems with this way of thinking. To begin with, an analysis of the social realities reveals that the socially created sexual differences tend in fact to matter the most.

Sex-role differentiation, not gender per se, makes men and women as different as they are from each other, and sex-role differences are invoked to justify most sexual differentiation at any of the levels of society.

More importantly, even if naturally occurring sexual differences were of such a nature that they were of obvious prima facie social relevance, this would by no means settle the question of whether in the good society sex should or should not be as minimally significant as eye color. Even though there are biological differences between men and women in nature, this fact does not determine the question of what the good society can and should make of these differences. I have difficulty understanding why so many persons seem to think that it settles the question adversely to anything like the assimilationist ideal. They might think so for two different reasons. In the first place, they might think the differences are of such a character that they substantially affect what would be possible within a good society. Just as the fact that humans are mortal necessarily limits the features of any possible good society, so, they might argue, the fact that males and females are physiologically different limits the features of any possible good society.

In the second place, they might think the differences are of such a character that they are relevant to the question of what would be desirable in the good society. That is to say, they might not think that the differences determine to a substantial degree what is possible, but that the differences ought to be taken into account in any rational construction of an ideal social existence.

The second reason seems to me to be a good deal more plausible than the first. There appear to be very few, if any, respects in which the ineradicable, naturally occurring differences between males and females must be taken into account. The industrial revolution has certainly made any of the general differences in strength between the sexes capable of being ignored by the good society in virtually all activities. And sex-role acculturation, not biology, mistakenly leads many persons to the view that women are both naturally and necessarily better suited than men to be assigned the primary responsibilities of child rearing. Indeed, the only fact that seems required to be taken into account is the fact that reproduction of the human species requires that the fetus develop *in utero* for a period of months. Sexual intercourse is not necessary, for artificial insemination is available. Neither marriage nor the family is required for conception or child rearing. Given the present state of medical knowledge and natural realities of female pregnancy, it is difficult to see why any important institutional or interpersonal arrangements must take into account the existing gender difference of *in utero* pregnancy.

But, as I have said, this still leaves wholly open the question of how much the good society ought to build upon any ineradicable gender differences to construct institutions which would maintain a substantial degree of sexual differentiation. The arguments are typically far less persuasive for doing so than they appear upon the initial statement of this possibility. Someone might argue that the fact of menstruation, for instance, could be used as a premise upon which to predicate different social roles for females than for males. But this could only plausibly be proposed if two things were true: first, that menstruation is debilitating to women and hence relevant to their social role even in a culture which did not teach women to view menstruation as a sign of uncleanliness or as a curse; and second, that the way in which menstruation necessarily affects some or all women is in fact related in an important way to the role in question. But even if both of these were true, it would still be an open question whether any sexual differentiation ought to be built upon these facts. The society could still elect to develop institutions that would nullify the effect of the natural differences. And suppose, for example, what seems implausible—that some or all women will not be able to perform a particular task while menstruating, for example, guard a border. It would be easy enough, if the society wanted to, to arrange for substitute guards for the women who were incapacitated. We know that persons are not good guards when they are sleepy, and we make arrangements so that persons alternate guard duty to avoid fatigue. The same could be done for menstruating women, even given the implausibly strong assumptions about menstruation. At the risk of belaboring the obvious, I think it is important to see that the case against the assimilationist ideal— if it is to be a good one—must rest on arguments which show why some other ideal would be preferable; it cannot plausibly rest on the claim that the other ideal is either necessary or inevitable.

There is, however, at least one more argument based upon nature, or at least the "natural," that is worth mentioning. Someone might argue that significant sex-role differentiation is natural not in the sense that it is biologically determined but only in the sense that it is a virtually universal phenomenon in human culture. By itself, this claim of universality, even if accurate, does not directly establish anything about the desirability or undesirability of any particular ideal. But it can be made into an argument by the addition of the proposition that where there is widespread, virtually universal social practice, there is probably some good or important purpose served by the practice. Hence, given the fact of sex-role differentiation in all, or almost all, cultures, we have some reason to think that substantial sex-role differentiation serves some important purpose for and in human society.

I see no reason to be impressed by this argument. The premise which turns the fact of sex-role differentiation into any kind of a strong reason for sex-role differentiation is the premise of conservatism. And it is no more convincing here than elsewhere. There are any number of practices that are typical and yet upon reflection seem without significant social purpose. Slavery was once such a practice; war perhaps still is.

More to the point, perhaps, the concept of "purpose" is ambiguous. It can mean in a descriptive sense "plays some role" or "is causally relevant." Or, it can mean in a prescriptive sense "does something desirable" or "has some useful function." If "purpose" is used descriptively in the conservative premise, then the argument says nothing about the continued desirability of sex-role differentiation or the assimilationist ideal. If "purpose" is used prescriptively in the conservative premise, then there is no reason to think that premise is true.

To put it another way, the question is whether it is desirable to have a society in which sex-role differences are to be retained at all. The straightforward way to think about that question is to ask what would be good and what would be bad about a society in which sex functioned as eye color does in our society. We can imagine what such a society would look like and how it would work. It is hard to see how our thinking is substantially advanced by reference to what has typically or always been the case. If it is true, as I think it is, that the sex-role differentiated societies we have had so far have tended to concentrate power in the hands of males, have developed institutions and ideologies that have perpetuated that concentration, and have restricted and prevented women from living the kinds of lives that persons ought to be able to live for themselves, then this says far more about what may be wrong with any nonassimilationist ideal than the conservative premise says about what may be right about that ideal.

Nor is this all that can be said in favor of the assimilationist ideal. It seems to me that the strongest affirmative moral argument on its behalf is that it provides for a kind of individual autonomy that a nonassimilationist society cannot attain. Any nonassimilationist society will have sex roles. Some of its institutions will distinguish between individuals by virtue of their gender, and any such society will necessarily teach the desirability of doing so. And any substantially nonassimilationist society will make one's sexual identity an important characteristic, so that there will be substantial psychological, role, and status differences between males and females. Even if these could be attained without the systemic dominance of one sex over the other, they would be objectionable on the ground that they necessarily impair an individual's ability to develop his or her own characteristics, talents, and capabilities to the fullest extent to which he or she might desire. Sex roles, and all that accompany them, necessarily impose limits—restrictions on what one can do, be, or become. As such, they are at least prima facie wrong.

To some degree, all role-differentiated living is restrictive in this sense. Perhaps, therefore, all role-differentation in society is to some degree troublesome, and perhaps all strongly role-differentiated societies are objectionable. But the case against sexual differentiation need not rest upon this more controversial point. For one thing that distinguishes sex roles from many other roles is that they are wholly involuntarily assumed. One has no choice whatsoever about whether one shall be born a male or female. And if it is a consequence of one's being born a male or a female that one's subsequent emotional, intellectual, and material development will be substantially controlled by this fact, then permanent and involuntarily assumed restraints have been imposed on the most central factors concerning the way one will shape and live one's life. The point to be emphasized is that this would necessarily be the case, even in the unlikely event that substantial sexual differentiation could be maintained without one sex or the other becoming dominant and developing institutions and an ideology to support that dominance.

I do not believe that all I have said in this section shows in any conclusive fashion the desirability of the assimilationist ideal in respect to sex. I have tried to show why some typical arguments against the assimilationist ideal are not persuasive, and why some of the central ones in support of that ideal are persuasive. But I have not provided a complete account or a complete analysis. At a minimum, what I have shown, I hope, is how thinking about this topic ought to proceed, and what kinds of arguments need to be marshalled and considered before a serious and informed discussion of alternative conceptions of a nonsexist society can even take place. Once assembled, these arguments need to be assessed individually and carefully before any final, reflective choice among the competing ideals can be made. There does, however, seem to be a strong presumptive case for something very close to, if not identical with, the assimilationist ideal.

INSTRUMENTALITIES

The instrumental perspective does not require a great deal of theoretical attention beyond what has already been said. It is concerned with the question of what would be the best way to move from the social realities to the ideal. The most salient considerations are, therefore, empirical ones—although of a complex sort.

The instrumental perspective is important for our purposes because all affirmative action programs are properly assessed from within this perspective. If the social reality is one of racial and sexual oppression—as I think it is—and if, for example, the most defensible picture of a nonracist, nonsexist society is the one captured by the assimilationist ideal, then the chief (and perhaps only) question to be asked of such programs is whether they are well suited to bring about movement from the existing state of affairs to a closer approximation of the assimilationist ideal. If it turns out, for example, that explicit racial quotas will in fact exacerbate racial prejudice and hostility, thereby making it harder rather than easier to achieve an assimilationist society, that is a reason which counts against the instrumental desirability of racial quotas. This would not settle the matter, of course, for there might also be respects in which racial quotas would advance the coming of the assimilationist society, for example, by redistributing wealth and positions of power and authority to blacks, thereby creating previously unavailable role models, as well as putting persons with different perspectives and interests in a position to influence more directly the course of social change.

But persons might be unhappy with this way of thinking about

affirmative action—and especially about affirmative action programs with quotas. They might have several different but related
objections. The first objection would be that there are more questions to be asked about means or instruments than whether they will
work to bring about a certain end. In particular, there is also the
question of the *way* they will work as means to bring about the end.
Some means may be morally objectionable as means, no matter
how noble or desirable the end.

I certainly agree with this general point. But the application to
particular cases, for example this one, vitiates the force of the objection. Indeed, given the way I have formulated the instrumental
perspective, I have left a good deal of room for the moral assessment of means to be built in. That is to say, I have described the
question as one of the instrumental "desirability" (not just the
"efficaciousness" in any narrow sense) of the means that are selected.

But still, someone might be dissatisfied and might say something
like this: it is wrong in principle ever to take an individual's race or
sex into account. Persons have a right never to have race or sex taken
into account. No reasons need be given; we just know they have that
right. This is a common way of talking today in moral philosophy,
but I find nothing persuasive or attractive about it. I do not know
that persons have such a right. I do not "see" or intuit the existence
of such a right. Instead, I think I can give and have given reasons
in my discussion of the social realities as well as my discussion of
the ideals for why they might be said to have rights not to be treated
in certain ways. That is to say, I have tried to show something of
what is wrong about the way blacks and women were and are
treated in our culture. I have not simply proclaimed the existence
of a right.

There is, however, another form of objection that is more convincing. The opponent of quotas and affirmative action programs
might argue that any proponent of these programs is guilty of intellectual inconsistency, if not racism or sexism. In times past, em-
ployers, universities, and many other social institutions did have
racial or sexual quotas (when they did not practice overt racial or
sexual exclusion), and it was clear that these quotas were pernicious.
What is more, many of those who most wanted to bring about the
eradication of those racial quotas are now untroubled by the new
programs which reinstitute them. This is just a terrible sort of in-

tellectual inconsistency which at worst panders to the fashion of the present moment and at best replaces intellectual honesty and integrity with understandable but misguided sympathy. The assimilationist ideal simply requires ignoring race and sex as relevant distinguishing features of people.

Such an argument is a useful means by which to bring out the way in which the analysis I am proposing can respond. The racial quotas and the practices of racial exclusion that were an integral part of the fabric of our culture, and which are still to some degree a part of it, were pernicious. They were a grievous wrong and it was and is important that all individuals concerned with being moral work for their eradication from our society. The racial quotas that are a part of contemporary affirmative action programs are, I think, commendable and right. But even if I am mistaken about the latter, the point to be gotten across is that there is no inconsistency involved in holding both views. For even if contemporary schemes of racial quotas are wrong, they are wrong for reasons very different from those that made quotas against blacks wrong.

As I have argued, the fundamental evil of programs that discriminated against blacks or women was that these programs were a part of a larger social universe which systematically maintained an unwarranted and unjust scheme which concentrated power, authority, and goods in the hands of white males. Programs which excluded or limited the access of blacks and women into these institutions were wrong both because of the direct consequences of these programs on the individuals most affected and because the system of racial and sexual superiority of which they were constituents was immoral in that it severely and without adequate justification restricted the capacities, autonomy, and happiness of members of the less favored categories.

Whatever may be wrong with today's affirmative action programs and quota systems, it should be clear that the evil, if any, is just not the same as that of the former system. Racial and sexual minorities do not constitute the dominant social group, nor do they define who is a fully developed member of the moral and social community. Quotas which prefer women or blacks do not add to the already relatively overabundant supply of resources and opportunities at the disposal of white males. If racial quotas are to be condemned or if affirmative action programs are to be abandoned, it should be because they will not work well to achieve the desired result. It is not because they seek either to perpetuate an unjust society or to realize a corrupt ideal.

Still a third version of this objection might be that when used in affirmative action programs the categories of race and sex are too broad in scope. They include some persons who do not have the appropriate characteristics and exclude some persons who do. If affirmative action programs made race and sex the sole criteria of selection, this would certainly be a plausible objection, although even here it is very important to see that the objection is no different in kind from that which applies to all legislation and rules. For example, in restricting the franchise to those who are eighteen and older, we exclude some who have all the relevant qualifications for voting and we include some who lack them. The fit can never be precise. But affirmative action programs almost always make race or sex a relevant condition, not a conclusive one. As such, they function the way all other classificatory schemes do. The defect, if there is one, is generic and not peculiar to programs such as these.

There is finally this objection: that affirmative action programs are wrong because they take race and sex into account rather than the only thing that matters—an individual's qualifications. Someone might argue that what is wrong with these programs is that they ignore persons who are more qualified by bestowing benefits on those who are less qualified in virtue of their being either black or female.

There are, I think, a number of things wrong with this objection, and not the least of them is that we do not live in a society in which there is even the serious pretense of a qualification requirement for many jobs of substantial power and authority. Would anyone claim that judges are chosen because they are the most qualified lawyers or the most qualified persons to be judges? Would anyone claim that Henry Ford II is the head of the Ford Motor Company because he is the most qualified person for the job? Or that the one hundred men who are senators are the most qualified persons to be senators? Part of what is wrong with even talking about qualifications and merit is that the argument derives some of its force from the erroneous notion that we would have a meritocracy were it not for affirmative action.

But there is a theoretical difficulty as well, one which cuts much more deeply into the argument about qualifications. To begin with, the person who favors "pure qualifications" cannot argue that the most qualified ought to be selected because the most qualified will perform most efficiently, since this appeal to efficiency was precisely what the opponent of affirmative action thought was wrong with taking the instrumental perspective in the first place. So to be at all persuasive, the argument for qualifications must be that those who are the most qualified *deserve* to receive the benefits (the job, the place in law school, etc.) because they are the most qualified. And the point here is that there is just no reason to think that this is correct. Let us consider more closely one case, that of preferential treatment in respect to admission to college or graduate school. There is a logical gap in the inference from the claim that a person is most qualified to perform a task, for example, to be a good student, to the conclusion that he or she deserves to be admitted as a student. Of course, those who deserve to be admitted should be admitted. But why do the most qualified deserve anything? There is simply no necessary connection between academic merit (in the sense of qualification) and deserving to be a member of a student body. Suppose, for instance, that there is only one tennis court in the community. Is it clear that the two best tennis players ought to be the ones permitted to use it? Why not those who were there first? Or those who will enjoy playing the most? Or those who are the worst and therefore need the greatest opportunity to practice? Or those who have the chance to play least frequently?

We might, of course, have a rule that says that the best tennis players get to use the court before the others. Under such a rule the best players would deserve the court more than the poorer ones. But that is just to push the inquiry back one stage. Is there any reason to think that we ought to have a rule giving good tennis players such a preference? Indeed many and varied arguments might be given for or against such a rule. And few if any of the arguments that might support the rule would depend upon a connection between ability and desert.

Someone might reply that the most able students deserve to be admitted to the university because all of their earlier schooling was a kind of competition, with university admission being the prize awarded to the winners. They deserve to be admitted because that is what the rule of the competition provides. In addition, it might be argued, it would be unfair now to exclude them in favor of others, given the reasonable expectations they developed about the way in which their industry and performance would be re-

warded. Minority admission programs, which inevitably prefer some who are less qualified over some who are more qualified, all possess this flaw.

There are several problems with this argument. The most substantial of them is that it is an empirically implausible picture of our social world. Most of what are regarded as the decisive characteristics for higher education have a great deal to do with things over which the individual has neither control nor responsibility: such things as home environment, socioeconomic class of parents, and, of course, the quality of the primary and secondary schools attended. Since individuals do not deserve having had any of these things more than any other individuals, they do not, for the most part, deserve their qualifications. And since they do not deserve their abilities they do not in any strong sense deserve to be admitted because of their abilities.

To be sure, if there has been a rule which connects, say, performance at high school with admission to college, then there is a weak sense in which those who do well at high school deserve, for that reason alone, to be admitted to college. In addition, if persons have built up or relied upon their reasonable expectations concerning performance and admission, they have a claim to be admitted on this ground as well. But it is certainly not obvious that these claims of desert are any stronger or more compelling than competing claims based upon the needs of or advantages to women or blacks from programs of preferential treatment. And as I have indicated, all rule-based claims of desert are weak or contingent claims unless and until the rule which creates the claim is itself shown to be a justified one.

Finally, I hasten to acknowledge that qualifications are also potentially relevant in at least three other respects. In the first place, there is some minimal set of qualifications without which the benefits of participation in higher education cannot be obtained by the individuals involved. In the second place, the qualifications of the students within the university will affect to some degree or other the benefits obtainable to anyone within it. And finally, the qualifications of students within the university may also affect the way the university functions in respect to the rest of the world. The university will do some things better and some things worse, depending upon the qualifications of those who make it up. If the students are "less qualified," teachers may have to spend more time with them and less time on research. Some teachers may find teaching now more interesting. Others may find it less so. But all these considerations only establish that qualifications, in this sense, are relevant, not that they are decisive. This is wholly consistent with the claim that minority group membership is also a relevant but not decisive consideration when it comes to matters of admission. And that is all that initially any preferential treatment program—even one with quotas—has ever tried to do.

I do not think I have shown programs of preferential treatment to be right and desirable, for I have not sought to answer all of the empirical questions that may be relevant. But I have, I hope, shown that it is wrong to think that contemporary affirmative action programs are racist or sexist in the centrally important sense in which many past and present features of our society have been and are racist and sexist. The social realities do make a fundamental difference. It is also wrong to think that these programs are in any strong sense either unjust or unprincipled. The case for programs of preferential treatment can plausibly rest both on the view that such programs are not unfair to white males (except in the weak, rule-dependent sense described above) and on the view that it is unfair to continue the present set of unjust—often racist and sexist—institutions that compose the social reality. The case for these programs also rests on the thesis that it is fair, given the distribution of power and influence in the United States, to redistribute in this way, and that such programs may reasonably be viewed as useful means by which to achieve very significant social ideals.

CONCLUSION

I do not think that the topics of racism, sexism, and preferential treatment are easily penetrable. Indeed, I have tried to show that they contain complicated issues which must be carefully distinguished and discussed. But I also believe, and have tried to show, that the topics are susceptible to rational analysis. There is a difference beween problems that are difficult because of confusion, and problems that are difficult because a number of distinct ideas and arguments must be considered. It is my ambition to have moved thinking about the topics and issues in question some distance from the first to the second of these categories.

IV

Is More Choice Better Than Less?[1]

Gerald Dworkin

IN RECENT YEARS THE WAYS OF THINKING practiced by economists
have provided the theoretical apparatus for attempting to clarify
and resolve normative problems in a number of areas of social policy. Among the areas in which fruitful work has been done are tort
theory, voting behavior, constitutional choice, criminal justice, and
the theory of property rights. At the same time, of course, economists
have applied the tools of welfare economics to problems of allocation of resources in areas such as education, health, consumer
choice, insurance, and natural resources.

In all of these areas—both traditional and new—two kinds of
tasks are at issue. One is the descriptive task of trying to explain
various phenomena: why rules of liability are the way they are, or
why they change over time, why a system of private property arose,
why individuals make certain choices in the marketplace. The other
task is to assist in answering various normative questions: Should
manufacturers of various products be held strictly liable for accidents caused by defects? Ought blood to be collected on a market or
volunteer basis? Should gasoline be rationed or should prices be allowed to rise until the market is cleared? Ought income to be redis-
tributed? Should need alone determine the distribution of medical
care? Is it better to have a volunteer or conscript army? What justifies a progressive rate of taxation on incomes? Ought people to be

1. Versions of this paper were read to the Philosophy Departments of
New York University, University of Wisconsin, Northwestern University,
University of Florida, and Georgetown University. It was also given as an
address to the Mountain-Plains Philosophical Association. In addition to the
members of these audiences, I am grateful to Joshua Rabinowitz, Lawrence
Crocker, Huntington Terrell, and Jane English for written comments.

compensated for losses arising from externalities in the existing system of property rights? These are all important and difficult problems, and a mode of analysis which promises us help—if not solutions—in thinking about them is surely to be welcomed.

It would seem, however, that a mode of analysis which has normative implications must contain, either explicitly or implicitly, normative assumptions. Economists, who are well aware of this issue, have been better than most people in trying to make explicit exactly what their criteria of better and worse are, and the states of affairs to which they attribute value. I wish in this essay to examine an assumption that plays a key role in many policy debates but which has received little critical scrutiny—the view that for the rational individual more choices are always preferable to fewer.

MORE CHOICES AS A SUPPORT FOR PUBLIC POLICY

Let me first give some examples of how this postulate is used to argue for various policy decisions.

Gordon Tullock uses the principle in an argument justifying the inheritance of wealth.[2] Assuming Pareto optimality (someone is made better off and no one is made worse off) as a normative criterion, Tullock argues that the wealth-holder is made better off since he has an option which he would not have if inheritances were not allowed.

A similar argument is made by economists to argue the superiority of income redistribution by means of cash transfers rather than "in kind" provision of various goods, such as food stamps or medical care. The argument again relies on the view that if the recipient receives cash he can spend it on the particular good in question or choose an alternative expenditure, whereas he has no such choice if he receives the good itself.[3]

---

2. Gordon Tullock, "Inheritance Justified," *Journal of Law and Economics* 14 (1971): 465.

3. This, of course, is only true if there is no subsequent trade possible. But, in the case of many goods considered for redistribution (e. g., education, health), this is usually the case. Cf. E. O. Olsen, "Some Theorems in the Theory of Efficient Transfers," *Journal of Political Economy* 79 (1971): 166–76. For a counter-view see Lester Thurow, "Government Expenditures: Cash or In-Kind Aid?" in *Markets and Morals*, edited by Gerald Dworkin, Gordon Bermant, and Peter G. Brown, (New York: Hemisphere Publishing, 1977), pp. 85–106.

Again, with respect to the issue of how blood should be collected, Arrow argues against Titmuss's claim that blood should not be purchased. "Economists typically take for granted that since the creation of a market increases the individual's area of choice it therefore leads to higher benefits. Thus, if to a voluntary blood system we add the possibility of selling blood, we have only expanded the individual's range of alternatives. If he derives satisfaction from giving, it is argued, he can still give, and nothing has been done to impair that right."[4]

The clearest statement of the assumption on the theoretical level by an economist is found in *The Logic of the Law*, by Gordon Tullock. In a chapter entitled "Fundamental Assumptions" his third "basic postulate" is that "an individual would prefer to be permitted to choose . . . that an individual would always prefer to have his range of choices widened."[5]

The view that more choices are preferable to fewer is shared not only by economists but by many political philosophers. Interestingly, it is shared by philosophers who come to rather different conclusions on substantive matters. Thus, both Rawls and Nozick accept the thesis. Rawls classifies liberty as a primary good, that is, one which any rational man will prefer more of to less. His reasoning is that individuals "are not compelled to accept more if they do not wish to, nor does a person suffer from a greater liberty."[6] Nozick uses the claim as part of an argument designed to distinguish offers from threats in terms of their effect on liberty. His contention is that "rational man would be willing to move and to choose to move from the preoffer to the offer situation, whereas he would normally not be willing to move or to choose to move from the prethreat situation to the threat situation."[7] This is equivalent to asserting that a rational man always prefers to be offered expanded choices.

4. Kenneth Arrow, "Gifts and Exchanges," *Philosophy and Public Affairs* I (1972): 349–50.

5. Gordon Tullock, *The Logic of the Law* (New York: Basic Books, 1971), pp. 15, 18.

6. John Rawls, *A Theory of Justice* (Cambridge: Harvard Univ. Pr., 1972), p. 143.

7. Robert Nozick, "Coercion," in *Philosophy, Politics and Society*, 4th Series, edited by Peter Laslett, Walter G. Runciman, and Quentin Skinner, (Oxford: Blackwell, 1967), p. 132. While Nozick believes there are exceptions he thinks that all such cases can be analyzed in terms of a special context or

Let us consider what Mill labels (in a different context) "the very large and conspicuous exceptions" to this principle.[8] By doing so we shall not only determine more exactly the limits of the principle, but also, hopefully, achieve a better understanding of its justification in those situations in which it does apply.

MORE CHOICES PREFERABLE TO FEWER

Let me begin by trying to make clear the thesis that more choices are always preferable to fewer. First, when one speaks of more choices the idea is that one has an original set of choices (which may be zero) and at least one choice is added. We are not considering the case where we have some partially disjoint set which happens to have a larger number of choices than the first. Obviously, having a choice between the Budapest and the Guarneri is preferable to a choice among all the amateur string quartets in New York City.

Next, it does not count against the thesis if additional choices make it less likely that one will get what one wants than if one only had the initial set of choices. Thus, if one is faced with the famous two doors behind which are the lady and the tiger, one does not want one's choices increased by adding three more doors behind all of which are tigers. The thesis must be understood as referring to choices in which the outcome is known.

Finally, the thesis must be understood as having some implicit "other things being equal" clause. Suppose, for example, A says to B that if B is offered more options with respect to some matter, then A will kill B. Here what makes B shun additional choices has nothing to do with the nature of the choices or the nature of choosing but rather an arbitrary cost attached to the choices. The presence of this cost is too contingent to count against the choices.

RELEVANT EXCEPTIONS TO THE MORE CHOICES PRINCIPLE

I shall present cases in which more choice is not to be desired and where the connection between the additional choices and the "costs" reflects either general features of choice or intrinsic features of particular choices.

---

the presence of some extraneous reasons. Cf. Gerald Dworkin, "Acting Freely," *Nous* 4 (1970): 367–83.

8. J. S. Mill, *Principles of Political Economy* (New York: Kelley, 1900), 2: 488. Mill is referring to the "obvious" principle that each person is the best judge of his own interest.

Decision-making costs

Much recent economic literature has focused attention on the concept of transaction costs. It is now generally recognized that the formation and perpetuation of various forms of market exchange is not costless. Also, the size of such costs must enter into an assessment of whether markets or other forms of resource allocation are most efficient. It should also be recognized that the making of choices is not a costless activity and that the assessment of whether one's welfare is improved by having a wider range of choices is often dependent upon an assessment of the costs involved in having to make those choices.

The kinds of costs are quite varied and I am going to suggest some samples rather than a precisely stated typology. One of the most obvious costs is that of acquiring the information required to make reasonable choices, for the notion of rationality is tied very closely to the notion of a well-informed choice. The proliferation of products, services, etc., hailed with much enthusiasm as the chief virtue of competitive markets, brings with it the need to know more and more in order to make intelligent choices. Henry Ford was said to have offered his customers a choice of colors—black. This undoubtedly restricted the range a customer had to choose from but it also eliminated the need to answer questions such as: Which color is the safest in terms of visibility? Which color is likely to show the least dirt? Which color is my spouse likely to prefer? Which color will last in terms of fashion? The example is a trivial one. When it comes to questions of product safety, or a doctor's competence, or the consequences of going to a particular college, the issues become more serious, the information more difficult to obtain, and the costs of acquiring the information higher.[9]

In addition to the costs of acquiring relevant information there are the costs in time and effort of making the choices. Anybody who has tried to buy a house or a car will be aware of the time-consuming nature of these choices. And while one can trade off money for time by hiring agents to do the initial screening, the nature of the choice dictates a necessary investment of personal time.

9. There are various ways in which the law may eliminate the need for acquiring information. One can embody certain information in the product itself, e. g., by setting product standards; or, by banning products from the market, the consumer can be spared the task of making comparisons.

One does not want to live in a house picked out by a real estate agent.[10]

There are, in addition, the psychic costs of having made the decision. "Was this really the right house or college or doctor?" "If I had waited would I have had a better selection, a cheaper price?" "Since it's my choice how does it reflect on me?" This last worry brings us to the next category of reasons that weigh on the side of preferring fewer choices—the issue of responsibility.

Responsibility for choice

At the most fundamental level responsibility arises when one acts to bring about changes in the world as opposed to letting fate or chance or the decisions of others determine the future. Indeed, once I am aware that I have a choice my failure to choose now counts against me. I can now be held responsible for events which, prior to the possibility of choosing, were not attributable to me. And with the fact of responsibility comes the pressure (social and legal) to make "responsible" choices.

Let us consider a specific instance which has arisen recently. Medical advances have made it possible, by the technique of amniocentesis, to determine whether the fetus a woman bears is normal or is genetically deficient in a number of ways. Conjoined with this new knowledge has come the removal of legal restrictions on the right of a woman to have an abortion, at least in the first twenty-four weeks of gestation. These two circumstances now imply that if a woman brings, say, a Down's syndrome infant into the world, she (and the father) bear the responsibility for this action; this responsibility could not have been attributed to them prior to the possibility of determining the normality of the fetus and the legal possibility of terminating the pregnancy. Now, both in her own mind and in the minds of those who are aware of her decision, she must assume responsibility for the correctness of her choice. The defective child—if she chooses to bear it—can no longer be viewed as inevitable bad luck or as an act of God or as a curse.

Without going to the metaphysical leap of a "fear of freedom" we can on a more sober level accept the fact that more choices

10. One of the roles of social conventions (norms of greeting, modes of acceptable dress) is to eliminate the necessity of making choices. Wittgenstein is said to have told his landlady that he did not care what he had for breakfast as long as it was the same thing every day.

bring in their train more responsibility, and that these are costs which must be taken into account. In addition to bearing the responsibility in one's own mind, there arises the possibility of being held responsible.[11]

Pressures to conform

The fact that one has new possibilities for choice opens the possibility of social and legal sanctions being brought to bear on the maker of the choice. Consider, for example, the possibility of predetermining the sex of one's children. This possibility is now at hand in a negative fashion—amniocentesis plus abortion of the fetus, if it is of the undesired sex—and will soon be possible in a positive fashion (techniques for separating the male-producing sperm from female ones). Leaving aside for the moment the question of the adverse effects on society such choices might cause— the available evidence from surveys of parental preference is that a surplus of males would be produced—consider the social pressures that are likely to be exerted on parents to produce one sex rather than the other (for example, the grandparents who always wanted a little girl, or the community which needs more soldiers).

A rather different example of the same phenomenon occurs in many university communities with respect to the issue of coed dormitories and cohabitation. The traditional libertarian response to this question has been a reference to freedom of choice. Those who wish to cohabit now can, while those who do not wish to can continue in their (old fashioned?) ways. The opening of new options cannot be harmful and is beneficial to some. But this ignores the sociology of the situation. The obvious reply—which came fairly quickly from those who felt the pressures of their peers— is that by allowing cohabitation, the social pressures from one's peers to act in a similar fashion increased and the easy excuse formerly available to the uninclined vanishes. Similarly, one of the justifications for making duelling illegal is that unless this is done

---

11. Cf. the reasoning behind one court's decision to force a Jehovah's Witness to have a lifesaving blood transfusion. The court argued, on a fine point of theology, that the religious freedom of the patient was not inhibited, since it was the *choice* of blood, not the blood itself, which was forbidden. *Application of the President and Directors of Georgetown College*, 331 F. 2d 1000 (D. C. Cir.), *Cert denied*, 377 U. S. 978 (1964). William Powers reminded me of this decision.

individuals might be forced to manifest their courage and integrity in ways which they would wish to avoid.

As another example consider the argument of Tullock that allowing the inheritance of wealth is a Pareto optimal policy.[12] Leaving aside the obvious objections (the inequality of opportunity, etc.) which he considers, there is the objection that the wealth holder himself may be worse off by having the option. He might prefer to spend all his wealth on himself and leave none to his heirs. A law which denies him the option of leaving his money to others frees him from the expectations and pressures of others.

I am not now arguing that the existence of various pressures to conform should be taken as decisive in retaining the status quo. It may be argued that, either because people have a right to such increased choices or because it is simply desirable to do so, such pressures have to be tolerated. I am simply pointing out the ways in which increased choices may incur costs. In particular one of the costs may be, as above, a decrease in the likelihood of exercising previous choices. I turn now to this category.

Decreasing likelihood of exercising previous choices

I quoted in the introduction Arrow's argument in favor of allowing a market for blood ". . . if to a voluntary blood donor system we add the possibility of selling blood, we have only expanded the individual's range of alternatives. If he derives satisfaction from giving he can still give, and nothing has been done to impair that right."[13] Richard Titmuss in his essay on this subject, "The Gift Relationship," argues that this is false. The argument is not a clear one and it is worth some time pursuing it since the general point is one relevant to our topic. Titmuss states ". . . private market systems in the United States and other countries not only deprive men of their freedom to choose to give or not to give but by so doing escalate other coercive forces in the social system which lead to the denial of other freedoms. . . . We believe that policy and processes should enable men to be free to choose to give to unnamed strangers. They should not be coerced or constrained by the market."[14] The question which Arrow raises is how can expanding choices

12. Tullock, "Inheritance Justified," *The Logic of Law*, pp. 465–74.
13. Arrow, "Gifts and Exchanges," p. 350.
14. Richard Titmuss, *The Gift Relationship* (New York: Random House, 1972), pp. 239, 242.

decrease them? How can being free to give or sell blood constitute a less free system than one in which one can only give blood (or for that matter only sell)? Peter Singer seems to interpret Titmuss's claim as being one about the liberty to give a certain kind of gift. "The right that Titmuss says is threatened is not a simple right to give, but the right to give 'in non-material as well as material ways.' This means not merely the right to give money for some commodity that can be bought or sold for a certain amount of money, but the right to give something that cannot be bought, that has no cash value, and must be given freely if it is to be obtained at all. This right, if it is a right—it would be better to say, this freedom—really is incompatible with the freedom to sell, and we cannot avoid denying one of these freedoms when we grant the other."[15] So freedom is diminished because prior to the introduction of the freedom to sell we were free to give something which cannot be purchased. Now we are only free to give something that can be purchased as well.

The argument strikes one as paradoxical. Suppose in a certain prison, mail could go out only after being read by a censor. New regulations allow the prisoner a choice of sending his mail out in the accustomed fashion or un-read by a censor. Surely we would regard this as an expansion of freedom. Yet a Singerian argument could be constructed to show that whereas previously a prisoner could send a letter knowing it would be read by the censor, now the nature of his letter is altered. The recipient of the letter is not guaranteed to have had the letter read by someone other than the writer of the letter. Of course the example is silly because we can think of no reason to want to be assured of this fact. But this seems to show that it is the alteration of the nature of the gift and not the effect on freedom that is crucial.

Let us put the point another way. We are not able to give a gift of a certain kind, and hence the issue of freedom does not arise. If I touch you, I make it impossible for anyone to speak to you while speaking to someone untouched by me. If we allow people to work on the Sabbath we make it impossible for anyone to work six days a week, and to be assured that everyone else will rest on the Sabbath. And people may want to have that assurance, just as they may want

15. Peter Singer, "Freedoms and Utilities in the Distribution of Health Care," in *Markets and Morals*, pp. 163–64.

to be able to give something that cannot be bought. But we should keep distinct the myriad of ways in which we can make things impossible to do from those very special restrictions which constitute enlarging or restricting freedom.

A more plausible way of defending Titmuss is Singer's later view that the argument should not be formulated in terms of a denial of freedom but rather in terms of the likely results that the expansion of choices will have on the motivation of individuals to continue to give voluntarily.

> The existence of a commercial system may discourage voluntary donors. It appears to discourage them, not because those who would otherwise have made voluntary donations choose to sell their blood instead if this alternative is available to them (donors and sellers are, in the main, different sections of the population) but because the fact that blood is available as a commodity, to be bought and sold, affects the nature of the gift that is made when blood is donated. . . . even if these people had the formal right to give to a voluntary program that existed alongside commercial blood banks, their gift would have lost much of its significance. . . . The fact that blood is a commodity, that if no one gives it, it can still be bought, makes altruism unnecessary, and so loosens the bonds that can otherwise exist between strangers in the community.[16]

So by changing the nature of what they are doing people are less likely to use the options they exercised in the past.

The effect of new options on the use of previous possibilities is present in many areas. Consider the effects of television on family life. Readers of nineteenth century novels will recall the many scenes depicting a family participating actively in their own cultural enrichment. Parents and children played music together, staged family reading, wrote and performed plays. It is not that families could not do such things today (some undoubtedly still do), but that the ready availability of effortless amusement at the touch of a switch makes the use of such options unlikely.

There are, of course, examples of situations in which it is not the willingness to exercise choices that is reduced but the choices themselves. Consider the development of the use of the automobile and its effect on mass transportation. At first the purchase of an auto-

16. Singer, "Freedoms and Utilities," pp. 161–62.

mobile greatly expanded the options open to individuals. They could take the bus to work or their car. They were not restricted to the particular schedules of mass transit. But as more and more people began to take advantage of the enlargement of options, funds were diverted from maintenance and improvement of mass transit to the construction of more and better highways. Powerful lobbies developed which encouraged the development of this process so that eventually many inhabitants of cities found themselves increasingly in the position of having to buy a car to get to work. The option of mass transit or private automobile had, in effect, been closed due to the decline of the former. What started out as an increase of the area of choice resulted in a situation in which one of the original choices was no longer available. While such cases are interesting they are irrelevant to the thesis since we do not have all of the original choices.

Increased choices that diminish welfare

We have been considering cases of the impact of choice-expansion on choice. When the choices lost are considered better or more important or more satisfying than the choices gained, a loss of welfare may have occurred. But welfare can be diminished in other ways than by loss or restriction of choices. I shall consider, briefly, some examples of welfare decline which are of this broader category.

Let me begin by considering an example which on the face of it would provide little reason to expect welfare decline—the choice between free and arranged marriages. Philip Slater points out an interesting consequence of abandoning arranged marriages.

> There is probably no arena in which free personal choice is more universally valued than that of marital selection, and certainly much misery and horror resulted from the imposition of cultural norms and parental wishes on reluctant brides and bridegrooms. At the same time it would be difficult to maintain that free choice has brought any substantial increase in marital bliss throughout the land. What was lost when people began to choose their own mates was serendipity. When the choice was made on purely practical, social or economic grounds there was an even chance that one might marry a person whose personality and interpersonal style would necessitate a restructuring of one's own neurotic patterns. The compulsive tendency people now have to reproduce their

childhood experiences in their marriages is jarred in such a system by the reality of the other person. While I would never advocate a return to the older system, we should be alert to its advantages as well as its more familiar drawbacks.[17]

One of the main arguments for supposing that more choices are always desirable is that adding additional options cannot make one worse off for one need not exercise any of the new choices. This is to ignore the fact that the possibility of increased choices can affect (for the worse) the original situation. Consider, for example, marriage as a social institution which may be dissolved (more or less easily) as compared to a situation in which the possibility of dissolution is not present. The presence or absence of this possibility must affect the expectations brought to the marriage, the ability to tolerate imperfections of the marriage partner, and the sense of commitment to the marriage. It is surely naive to suppose that the mere presence of a choice which need not be taken cannot alter the initial situation.

As another example, consider the following passage by Tibor Scitovsky.

> If, beginning with a situation in which only one kind of shirt were available, a man was transposed to another in which ten different kinds were offered to him, including the old kind, he could of course continue to buy the old kind of shirt. But it does not follow that, if he elects to do this, he is no worse off in the new situation. In the first place, he is aware that he is now *rejecting* nine different kinds of shirts whose qualities he has not compared. The decision to ignore the other nine shirts is itself a cost, and inasmuch as additional shirts continue to come on to the market, and some are withdrawn, he is being subjected to a continual process of decision-taking even though he is able, and willing, to buy the same shirt. In the second place, unless he is impervious to fashion, he will feel increasingly uncomfortable in the old shirt. It is more likely that he will be tempted, then, to risk spending an unpredictable amount of time and trouble in the hope of finding a more suitable shirt.[18]

In *The Sickness unto Death* Kierkegaard refers to the "despair of possibility," a situation in which possibility "appears to the self

17. Philip Slater, *Earthwalk* (New York: Anchor Pr., 1974), p. 17.
18. Tibor Scitovsky, *The Joyless Economy* (New York: Oxford Univ. Pr., 1976), p. 98.

ever greater and greater, more and more things become possible.
. . . At last it is as if everything were possible—but this is precisely
when the abyss has swallowed up the self."[19] Is it really the case
that for the rational among us it is never the case that "the soul
goes astray in possibility"?

As a last category of cases where increased choice may bring welfare decline there are often strategic reasons for not wanting certain
choices to be available. If a bank teller knows the combination to
the safe he can be threatened into opening it. If we have no choice
about whether to retaliate against nuclear attack (the "doomsday"
machine which responds automatically to our being attacked) then
our threat of retaliation is more credible than if we have such a
choice.

Linked choices and unlinked choices

If we turn to prisoners' dilemma situations we find an interesting category of adverse consequences of having certain choices. It
is well known that one way of avoiding the dilemma is to make it
impossible for either party to make its dominant choice. Having
fewer choices ensures that they will both be better off. But, it might
be replied, that what is most desirable for any particular player is
that the others be coerced into performing the dominated action
where he is left free to perform the dominant one. True enough; but,
as is the case for many kinds of social interaction, one often cannot remain exceptional. Some form of universal choice is required.
Choices come linked together rather than separate so that the question of whether the individual is to have more choices becomes the
same as whether some larger group is to have those choices as well.
While these cases are not, in theory, counter-examples to the thesis,
they are so in practice. When considerations of fairness or efficiency or political reality require that our choices be linked together, then it is impossible to ignore the effect on the individual
of others having the additional choices as well.

Failure to appreciate fully this fact undermines Rawls's argument for the status of liberty as a primary good, that is, one which
any rational person prefers more of to less. He says that individuals
"are not compelled to accept more if they do not wish to, nor does

19. *Fear and Trembling and The Sickness Unto Death*, trans. by Walter
Lowrie (Garden City: Doubleday, 1954), p. 169.

a person suffer from a greater liberty."[20] This is presumably on the grounds that we are all to have an equal liberty. But since, as he recognizes, the worth of liberty to various persons is not equal, then a larger liberty for all may leave some worse off than a smaller liberty for all.[21] As Hart states, "It does not follow that a liberty which can only be obtained by an individual at the price of its general distribution through society is one that a rational person would still want."[22]

There are other cases in which it is not the fact that choices are linked together which makes it rational for the individual to prefer less choice, but the fact that they are not so linked—that he is exceptional. It is not fair for some person to be able to purchase release from a system for conscription and so we do not allow the option. Again, it is a bad argument to say that it is still preferable from the standpoint of any particular individual to have such an option because, if he is motivated by moral considerations, he can always decline to exercise the option. This misses the point that it is already morally significant that he *has* the choice, whether or not he intends to make use of it. It is his having the choice, while others do not, which is ruled out on moral grounds.

Limiting choices for special moral relationships

An important kind of consideration, to which little attention has been paid, is the role of restricting choices in symbolizing or expressing moral relationships. Consider, for example, the notion of fidelity in a marriage. By foreclosing in advance the idea of alternative sexual relationships (foreclosing not by declining options but by abandoning the very idea of an option), one can express to one's partner the special character of one's relationship. The abandoning of certain choices provides a way of manifesting in the clearest fashion that the relationship is of a special nature.

This way of manifesting certain ideals can take place on a larger scale. I know of a philosophy department whose members have agreed not to use outside offers to raise their salaries. An individual

20. Rawls, *A Theory of Justice*, p. 143.

21. See my "Non-neutral Principles," *Journal of Philosophy* 71 (1974): 491–506, for an application of this reasoning to the problem of tolerance.

22. H. L. A. Hart, "Rawls on Liberty and Its Priority," *University of Chicago Law Review* 40 (1973): 551.

who might otherwise benefit by use of the market can, by renouncing this option in advance, express a certain notion of community solidarity.

Note that in these cases it need not be argued that these are the only ways of expressing such ideals. One can conceive of a community (of philosophers or others) who do not regard their community as undermined by the fact that individuals through either talent or luck are enabled to better their circumstances. But that such commitments are one way of expressing the unique character of a community, and that it may be perfectly rational to do so, cannot be denied.

Paternalism

Finally we come to a set of reasons for rejecting more choices which I have discussed at some length in an earlier paper.[23] These are cases where it is rational for the individual to reject the possibility of making certain choices on the grounds that if he had the choices he would be tempted to make them and he recognizes, in advance, that making such choices would be harmful in terms of his long-range interests.[24] The application of this line of reasoning to drug legislation, civil commitment procedures, and social security provisions, are obvious.

It need not be supposed that we always fear being swept away by strong emotions when we welcome having choices reduced. We may simply fear mistake or error. I would not want to have a bomb connected to a number I could dial on my phone because I might dial it by mistake.

23. Gerald Dworkin, "Paternalism," *Monist* 56 (1972): 64–84.
24. Rational chickens apparently act similarly. George Ainslie at Harvard has performed the following experiment: faced with a key that allowed them 1.5 seconds of food if they pecked at it when it turned red, or 4 seconds if they refrained from pecking, the chickens pecked. Ainslie then introduced a new contingency. The key would turn white about 11 seconds before it turned red, and if the chickens pecked the key when it was white, this prevented the key from turning red and they would obtain the 4-second reward. A peck on the white key prevented a choice between a small immediate reward and a large delayed one. The chickens pecked the white key about 90 per cent of the time it was offered to them. See H. Rachlin, *Introduction to Modern Behaviorism* (San Francisco: W. H. Freeman, 1970), pp. 186–88.

LIMITATIONS UPON THE FEWER CHOICES PRINCIPLE

A good deal has been said about the specific kinds of considerations which might lead individuals to prefer not having certain choices to having them; now, some reservations should be noted.

First, it does not follow that although individuals might under certain conditions prefer not to have had a certain choice, that having such choices they would (or should) refrain from exercising them. It could be rational to exercise the choice for a number of different reasons. It might be dangerous not to. While I might prefer that the speed limit be limited to fifty-five miles per hour, if in fact it is seventy and everyone else is driving at that speed, it might be folly not to exercise my choice on this matter. Considerations of "second-best" might bring it about that while it would be more just for none to have such choices, efforts by individuals to reject such choices (given their presence) might make a bad situation worse. One such example might be that of pacifism. In the ideal situation, no individual would have the option of using force to attain his ends (even where those ends are self-defense), but given that some individuals are going to exercise the option of using force in certain situations, for good persons to renounce that option would be to make a bad situation intolerable. It follows that it may be perfectly rational for individuals to resist having certain choices taken away even if they would have preferred not to have had such liberties in the first place.

Second, while some of my examples involved the state as the instrument of limiting choices, nothing I have said commits me to believing that it is the most appropriate instrument for such purposes. In many cases individuals can work out specific arrangements with friends, or make use of various market mechanisms for restricting choice (contracts), or use ingenious devices (such as the cigarette box with a lock and timer designed by Azrin to reduce smoking). The question of the appropriate mechanism for limiting choices can be decided only when given knowledge of the particular choices, the nature of the individuals involved, the administrative costs, and so forth.

Third, and related to this last point, from the fact that in some particular case it would be rational for the agent to have his choice restricted, it does not follow that others may do this for him against his will. The question of what is in the best interests of the individual is relevant to deciding issues of when coercion is justified, but it is by no means conclusive. A decent respect for the autonomy of individuals will make us very wary of limiting choices even when it is in the rational self-interest of the individuals concerned.

I hope that these counter-examples have shown the inadequacy of the thesis that more choice is always preferable to less. I want to close by looking at some of the reasons one might give for valuing choice and to argue that they do not lend support to the thesis.

INSTRUMENTAL AND INTRINSIC VALUE OF CHOICES

Arguments for the value of choice may rely either on the instrumental value of choices or on the instrinsic value. Instrumental value is enhanced when the greater number of choices contributes causally to the obtaining of other good things. Intrinsic value is increased when having more choices for its own sake is better than having fewer. I shall consider each in turn.

One of the ways in which increased choice contributes to the welfare of individuals is by increasing the probability that they will satisfy their desires. People want various things—goods and services, status, affection, power, health, security—and their chances of getting these things are often enhanced if they have more options to choose among. My chance of finding a shirt I like is greater if I have ten different shirts to choose among than if I have only two.

This is a contingent fact about the world. If my taste in shirts were such that I were indifferent to their fit, style, color, etc., greater choice would not increase the probability of my satisfying my desires. Similarly, even if I had rather strict requirements in a shirt but it just so happened that most shirts met those requirements, then again I would not value choice for its contribution to the satisfaction of my desires. But given the relatively bad fit between people's wishes and the objects of their satisfaction one is well advised to have a broader rather than narrower range of options. So one reason for wanting choices increased is the belief or hope that among the additional choices there will be something preferable to those things available among the existing choices.

Suppose, then, that existing choices provided me with items that optimally matched my preferences. Additional options simply provide the necessity for rejections. Would the instrumental value of increased choices be nil? No, for my preferences may change and the greater choices may then provide me with better means to satisfy my changed preferences. Right now I do not care about the presence or absence of rhubarb on the menu because I detest rhubarb. But I have been known to change my food preferences in the past, and if they change in favor of rhubarb I will be glad if rhubarb is an option. In addition, one way in which our preferences change is by noting unused options and trying them experimentally. That's how I discovered I liked scungilli.

There are other instrumental reasons for prefering more choices. Some people get satisfaction out of exercising choice; thinking about, choosing among, and making choices can be a source of satisfaction. Therefore, having more choices to exercise will provide increased satisfaction. Another reason for preferring more choice is that one wishes to develop certain character traits and their development requires that one practice by making choices. If one wants to develop self-confidence one may have to make choices rather than to remain passive.

A different kind of reason for wanting to make choices is to learn certain things about oneself. If one wants to discover whether one is rash or timid, courageous or cowardly, one can only do so by seeing what kinds of choices one makes in certain situations.

I do not see, however, that such considerations can lend support to anything other than an empirical generalization to the effect that in many (most? almost all?) circumstances we would prefer to be offered more options rather than less, since this will usually promote the attainment of desired goods. But this is no more than a rule of thumb, a rough guide to the future based on past experience. In a similar way I might reason that usually I am better off having more information. But if someone were to inform me that tomorrow I will be given a piece of new information I had not known before, then I have no firm conviction that this will be a good thing or a bad thing. It will all depend on whether I have some reason for wanting to know this new information—and I can certainly think of lots of reasons why I might be indifferent or even prefer not to know it.

The support of the stronger claim must come from the view that choice has intrinsic value, is desirable for its own sake. For if choice has value in virtue of being choice, then more of it must have more value. Leaving aside for the moment the antecedent of this claim, what is the logic of this argument? Does it really follow from the fact that having a child is (in part) intrinsically valuable, that having two is better? It certainly does not follow that if A is intrinsically valuable and B is intrinsically valuable that having A and B together is intrinsically valuable. Let A equal listening to a Bach partita and B equal listening to a Beethoven string quartet.

In any case here is a "proof" that having choices cannot be intrinsically valuable. Suppose someone ranks three goods A, B, and C in that order. Then, making certain plausible assumptions about the infinite divisibility of utility, there will be A, B, and C such that the person prefers a choice between B and C to receiving A. This will occur whenever the utility of having a choice between B and C plus the utility of B is greater than the utility of A. This seems to me irrational. Leaving aside some special feature about this particular choice, for example that somebody promised me $1,000 if I made the choice between B and C, why should I prefer to receive my second-ranked alternative to my first?

What does have intrinsic value is not having choices but being recognized as the kind of creature who is capable of making choices. That capacity underlies our idea of what it is to be a person and a moral agent worthy of respect by all. But, of course, the view that it is intrinsically better to be a creature that makes choices is consistent with the view that it is not always an improvement to have more.

Another noninstrumental value which attaches to being able to make choices is their constitutive value. By this I mean a value which resides neither in the causal effects of making choices nor in the value of choices for their own sake but as definitive of a larger complex which is itself valued. If one wants to be the kind of person who makes decisions and accepts the responsibility for them, or who chooses and develops a life-plan, then choices are valued not for what they produce, nor for what they are in themselves, but as constitutive of a certain ideal of a good life. What makes a life *ours* is that it is shaped by our choices, is selected from alternatives; therefore choice is valued as a necessary part of a larger complex. But again this would at most support the view that with respect to a certain range of choices, it is desirable to have some options.

I conclude that neither the instrumental nor the noninstrumental value of having choices supports the view that more are always preferable to fewer. In the realm of choice, as in all others, we must conclude—enough is enough.

V

The Child's Right to an Open Future
Joel Feinberg

HOW DO CHILDREN'S RIGHTS raise special philosophical problems?
Of course, not all rights of children have a distinctive character.
Many whole classes of rights are common to adults and children;
many are exclusive possessions of adults; perhaps none at all are
necessarily peculiar to children. In the common category are rights
not to be mistreated directly, for example, the right not to be
punched in the nose or to be stolen from. When a stranger slaps
a child and forcibly takes away his candy in order to eat it himself,
he has interfered wrongfully with the child's bodily and property
interests and violated his or her rights just as surely as if the ag-
gressor had punched an adult and forcibly helped himself to her
purse. Rights that are common to adults and children in this way
we can call "*A-C*–rights."

Among the rights thought to belong only to adults ("*A*–rights")
are the legal rights to vote, to imbibe, to stay out all night, and so
on. An interesting subpecies of these are those autonomy-rights
(protected liberties of choice) that could hardly apply to small children—the free exercise of one's religion, for example, which presupposes that one has religious convictions or preferences in the
first place. When parents choose to take their child to religious observances and to enroll him in a Sunday School, they are exercising
their religious rights, not (or not yet) those of the child.

The rights which I shall call "*C*–rights," while not strictly peculiar to children, are generally characteristic of them, and possessed by adults only in unusual or abnormal circumstances. Two
subclasses can be distinguished, and I mention the first only to dis-
miss it as not part of the subject matter of this essay, namely, those
rights that derive from the child's dependence upon others for the

basic instrumental goods of life—food, shelter, protection. Dependency-rights are common to all children, but not exclusive to them, of course, since some of them belong also to handicapped adults who are incapable of supporting themselves and must therefore be "treated as children" for the whole of their lives.

Another class of C–rights, those I shall call "rights-in-trust," look like adult autonomy rights of class A, except that the child cannot very well exercise his free choice until later when he is more fully formed and capable. When sophisticated autonomy rights are attributed to children who are clearly not yet capable of exercising them, their names refer to rights that are to be saved for the child until he is an adult, but which can be violated in advance, so to speak, before the child is even in a position to exercise them. Violations guarantee now that when the child is an autonomous adult, certain key options will already be closed to him. While he is still a child, he has the right to have these future options kept open until he is a fully formed self-determining agent capable of deciding among them. These "anticipatory autonomy rights" in class C are the children's rights in which I am most interested, since they raise the most interesting philosophical questions. They are, in effect, autonomy rights in the shape they must assume when held "prematurely" by children.

Put very generally, rights-in-trust can be summed up as the single "right to an open future," but of course that vague formula simply describes the form of the particular rights in question and not their specific content. It is plausible to ascribe to children a right to an open future only in some, not all respects, and the simple formula leaves those respects unspecified. The advantage of the general formula, however, is that it removes temptation to refer to certain rights of children by names that also apply to quite different rights of adults.[1] The adults's rights to exercise his religious

---

    1. John Locke preferred the more uniform usage according to which all human rights are A-C rights. In his usage, from which I here depart, we are all *born* with certain rights which we possess throughout our lives, from infancy through old age. Some of these rights, however, children cannot exercise, though they continue to possess them until they acquire the requisite capability. "Thus we are born free as we are born rational; not that we have actually the exercise of either; age that brings one, brings with it the other too." (*Second Treatise of Government*, Section 61). It would be a mistake to

beliefs, for example, is a class *A* right, but the right of the same name when applied to a small child is a right-in-trust, squarely in class *C*. One can avoid confusing the two by referring to the latter simply as part of the child's right to an open future (in respect to religious affiliation). In that general category it sits side by side with the right to walk freely down the public sidewalk as held by an infant of two months, still incapable of self-locomotion. One would violate that right in trust now, before it can even be exercised, by cutting off the child's legs. Some rights with general names are rather more difficult to classify, especially when attributed to older, only partly grown, children. Some of these appear to have one foot in class *A* and the other in the rights-in-trust subclass of the *C* category. For example, the right of free speech, interpreted as the freedom to express political opinions, when ascribed to a ten year old is perhaps mainly an actual *A*–right, but it is still partly a *C*–right-in-trust, at least in respect to those opinions which the child might one day come to form but which are presently beyond his ken.

People often speak of a child's "welfare" or his "interests." The interests protected by children's *A-C*–rights are those interests the child actually has now. Their advancement is, in a manner of speaking, a constituent of the child's good as a child right now. On the other hand the interests he might come to have as he grows up are the one's protected by his rights-in-trust of class *C*. While he is still a child, these future interests include those that he will in fact come to have in the future and also those he will never acquire, depending on the directions of his growth.

It is a truism among philosophers that interests are not the same things as present desires, with which they can, and often do, clash. Thus, if the violation of a child's autonomy right-in-trust can not

---

elevate this terminological difference into a philosophical quarrel. Obviously Locke can say everything in his terminology that I can in mine and *vice versa*. He was concerned with emphasizing the similarity in the moral status of children and adults, whereas this paper focuses on the differences. I have no objection if people talk about *A*-rights as if they are actually possessed by small infants (for example, the right to vote as one pleases) provided it is clearly understood that they are "possessed" in the sense that they are held in trust for the autonomous adults the children will (probably) become one day, and they are subject to violation now in a way that is *sui generis*.

always be established by checking the child's present interests, *a fortiori* it cannot be established by determining the child's present desires or preferences.[2] It is the adult he is to become who must exercise the choice—more exactly, the adult he will become if his basic options are kept open and his growth kept "natural" or unforced. In any case, that adult does not exist yet, and perhaps never will. But the child is potentially that adult, and it is that adult whose autonomy must be protected now (in advance).

When a mature adult has a conflict between getting what he wants now and having his options left open in the future, we are bound by our respect for his autonomy not to force his present choice in order to protect his future liberty. His present autonomy takes precedence even over his probable future good, and he may use it as he will, even at the expense of the future self he will one day become. Children are different. Respect for the child's future autonomy, as an adult, often requires preventing his free choice now. Thus the future self does not have as much moral weight in our treatment of adults as it does with children. Perhaps it should weigh as much with adults pondering their own decisions as it does with adults governing their own children. In the self-regarding case, the future self exerts its weight in the form of a claim to prudence, but prudence cannot rightly be imposed from the outside on an autonomous adult.

RIGHTS OF ADULTS AND CHILDREN IN CONFLICT

Moral perplexity about children's C–rights-in-trust is most likely to arise when those rights appear to conflict with certain A–rights of their parents, and the courts must adjudicate the conflict. Typically the conflict is between the child's protected personal interests in growth and development (rather than his immediate health or welfare) and the parents' right to control their child's upbringing, or to determine their own general style of life, or to practice their own religion free of outside interference. Very often the interests of the general community as represented by the state are involved too, for example, the concern that children not be a source of infection to others, that they grow up well enough informed to be responsible voting citizens, or that they not become criminal or

---

2. *Pace* William O. Douglas in his dissenting opinion in *Wisconsin v. Yoder*, 406 U.S. 205 (1972).

hopeless dependents on state welfare support. Thus custody hearings, neglect proceedings against parents, and criminal trials for violating compulsory school attendance laws and child labor statutes often become three-cornered contests among the rights of children, parents, and the state as representative of the collective interests of the community.[3] Sometimes, however, the community's interests are only marginally involved in the case, and the stark conflict between parent and child comes most clearly to the fore. Among the more difficult cases of this kind are those that pose a conflict between the religious rights of parents and their children's rights to an open future.

Children are not legally capable of defending their own future interests against present infringement by their parents, so that task must be performed for them, usually by the state in its role of *parens patriae*. American courts have long held that the state has "sovereign power of guardianship" over minors and other legally incompetent persons which confers upon it the right, or perhaps even the duty, to look after the interests of those who are incapable of protecting themselves. Mentally disordered adults, for example, who are deranged as to be unable to seek treatment for themselves, are entitled under the doctrine of *parens patriae* to psychiatric care under auspices of the state. Many mentally ill persons, however, are not cognitively deranged, and some of these do not wish to be confined and treated in mental hospitals. The government has no right to impose treatment on these persons, for the doctrine of *parens patriae* extends only to those unfortunates who are rendered literally incapable of deciding whether to seek medical treatment themselves; and even in these cases, the doctrine as liberally interpreted grants power to the state only to "decide for a man as we assume he would decide for himself if he were of sound mind."[4] When the courts must decide for children, however, as they presume the children themselves would (or will) when they are adults, their problems are vastly more difficult. As a general rule, the courts will not be so presumptuous as to speak now in the name of the future adult; but, on the other hand, there are some-

3. For illuminating analysis of these three-sided conflicts, see Stuart J. Baskin, "State Intrusion into Family Affairs: Justifications and Limitations," *Stanford Law Review* 26 (1974): 1383–1409.

4. John C. Roberts, "Civil Restraint, Mental Illness, and the Right to Treatment," *Yale Law Journal* 77 (1967): 87.

times ways of interfering with parents so as to postpone making serious and final commitments until the child grows to maturity and is legally capable of making them himself.

In 1944 in the case of *Prince v. Massachusetts* the U.S. Supreme Court upheld a Massachusetts statute that had been applied to prevent children of Jehovah's Witnesses from distributing religious pamphlets on the public streets in what their parents claimed was the free exercise of their religion.[5] The decision in this case has been severely criticized (and I think rightly) as a misapplication of the *parens patriae* doctrine,[6] but the Court's statement of that doctrine is unusually clear and trenchant. The state is concerned, said the court, not only with the immediate health and welfare of children but also with "the healthy, well-rounded growth of young people into full maturity as citizens with all that implies [in a democracy]. . . . Parents may be free to become martyrs themselves. But it does not follow that they are free in identical circumstances to make martyrs of their children before they have reached the age of full and legal discretion when they can make that decision for themselves."[7] It was no doubt an overstatement to describe the exposure of children to the apathy or scorn of passersby in the streets as "martyrdom," but the Court's well-stated but misapplied principle suggests other cases where religious liberty must retreat before the claims of children that they be permitted to reach maturity with as many open options, opportunities, and advantages as possible.

Twenty years later, in a quite different sort of case, a Long Island court upheld the religious rights of parents at the expense of their three small children. The twenty-four-year-old mother, injured in an automobile collision, was allowed to die when her husband refused on religious grounds to allow doctors to give her a blood transfusion. The husband, like his wife a member of Jehovah's Witnesses, remained adamant despite the pleadings of doctors. Finally the hospital administration appealed to State Supreme Court Judge William Sullivan, who refused to order the transfusion.

5. *Prince v. Massachusetts,* 321 U.S. 158 (1944).

6. See Justice Frank Murphy's dissenting opinion in *Prince,* and also Donald Giannella, "Religious Liberty, Nonestablishment, and Doctrinal Development," Pt. I, "The Religious Liberty Guarantee," *Harvard Law Review* 81 (1967): 1395.

7. *Prince v. Massachusetts,* pp. 168, 170.

It is too easy to criticize a judge who was forced to make a life or death decision in a legally difficult case on only a moment's notice, and I have no intention of doing so. On balance his decision might well have been justified even though the case for reading the scales in the children's favor was strong indeed. The three children, whose interests in present welfare and future development were directly involved, could not, of course, make the momentous decision for themselves, and both natural parents were determined to decide against the children's interests. Only the state in its capacity as protector of those who cannot help themselves (*parens patriae*) had the legal power to overrule the parents' decision. The religious beliefs of the parents were sincere and important; their contravention, according to the tenets of the parents' sect, would be serious sin, perhaps something akin to both cannibalism and adultery.[8] On the other balance pan was the diminished prospect of three children for a "healthy, well-rounded growth into full maturity" and their immediate and continuous need of maternal care and affection. The parents' "sin" would certainly be mitigated by the fact that it was committed involuntarily under governmental duress, whereas the children's deprivation, while perhaps being something short of "martyrdom," would be a permanent and possibly irreplaceable loss. On the other hand, some fathers might be able to replace their deceased wives quite effectively, either on their own or through prompt remarriage, so it is not perfectly clear that the case for applying the *parens patriae* doctrine in this instance ought to have been decisive.

Another close case, I think, but one where the interests of children do seem prior to the religious interests of their parents, was that in which the Kansas courts refused to permit an exemption for Amish communities from the requirement that all children be sent to state-accredited schools.[9] The Amish are descended from eighteenth century immigrants of strong Protestant conviction who settled in this country in order to organize self-sufficient farming communities along religious principles, free of interference from unsympathetic outsiders. There is perhaps no purer example of religious faith expressed in a whole way of life, of social organization

8. " 'If I allow blood to be given into her and if she lived, she wouldn't be considered my wife,' the police said Mr. Jackson had told the doctors."—*New York Times*, November 13, 1968.

9. *State v. Garber*, 197 Kan. 567, 419 P. 2d 896 (1966).

infused and saturated with religious principle. The aim of Amish education is to prepare the young for a life of industry and piety by transmitting to them the unchanged farming and household methods of their ancestors and a thorough distrust of modern techniques and styles that can only make life more complicated, soften character, and corrupt with worldliness. Accordingly, the Amish have always tried their best to insulate their communities from external influences, including the influence of state-operated schools. Their own schools teach only enough reading to make a lifetime of Bible study possible and only enough arithmetic to permit the keeping of budget books and records of simple commercial transactions. Four or five years of this, plus exercises in sociality, devotional instruction, inculcation of traditional virtues, and on-the-job training in simple crafts of field, shop, or kitchen, are all that is required, in a formal way, to prepare children for the traditional Amish way of life to which their parents are bound by the most solemn commitments.

More than this, however, was required by law of any accredited private school in the state of Kansas. Education is compulsory until the age of sixteen and must meet minimal curricular standards including courses in history, civics, literature, art, science, and mathematics more advanced than elementary arithmetic. Why not permit a limited exemption from these requirements out of respect for the constitutional right of the Amish to the free exercise of their religion and to the self-contained way of life that is inseparable from that exercise? The case for the exemption was strong. The Amish sincerity is beyond any question. The simple unworldly life that is part of their religion is prima facie inconsistent with modern education; and the virtues of simplicity and withdrawal are important, that is, more than merely incidental or peripheral to the Amish religion. Moreover, the small size of the Amish sect would minimize the effect of an exemption on the general educational level in Kansas. Indeed, insofar as there is a public interest involved in this problem (in addition to the clash of private interests) it seems to weigh more heavily on the Amish side of the scale, for as Mill pointed out in *On Liberty*, we all profit from the example of others' "experiments in living."[10] They permit us to choose our own way of life more aware of the various alternatives,

10. J. S. Mill, *On Liberty*, chap. 3, paragraphs 2, 3.

thus facilitating our own reasoning about such choices and reducing the possibility of error in our selection. Living examples of radically different ways of life constantly before our eyes cannot help but benefit all of us, if only by suggesting different directions in case our majority ways lead to dead ends.

The case against the exemption for the Amish must rest entirely on the rights of Amish children, which the state as *parens patriae* is sworn to protect. An education that renders a child fit for only one way of life forecloses irrevocably his other options. He may become a pious Amish farmer, but it will be difficult to the point of practical impossibility for him to become an engineer, a physician, a research scientist, a lawyer, or a business executive. The chances are good that inherited propensities will be stymied in a large number of cases, and in nearly all cases critical life-decisions will have been made irreversibly for a person well before he reaches the age of full discretion when he should be expected, in a free society, to make them himself. To be prepared for anything, including the worst, in this complex and uncertain world would seem to require as much knowledge as a child can absorb throughout his minority. These considerations have led many to speak of the American child's birth-right to as much education as may be available to him, a right no more valid than the religious rights of parents, but one which must be given reluctant priority in cases of unavoidable conflict.

Refusal to grant the exemption requested by the Amish only puts them in the same kind of position in respect to their children as all other parents. They are permitted and indeed expected to make every reasonable effort to transmit by example and precept their own values to their children. This is in fact a privileged position for parents, given their special relations of intimacy and affection with their children, even when compared to the rival influences of neighbors and schools; but still, in the interest of eventual full maturity, self-fulfillment, and natural many-sided development of the children themselves, parents must take their chances with outside influences.

The legal setback to the Amish at the hands of the Kansas Supreme Court was only temporary, however, and six years later in the case of *Wisconsin v. Yoder*[11] they won a resounding victory

11. *Wisconsin v. Yoder*, 406 U.S. 205 (1972).

in the Supreme Court of the United States. The Amish litigants in that case had been convicted of violating Wisconsin's compulsory school attendance law (which requires attendance until the age of sixteen) by refusing to send their children to public or accredited private school after they had graduated from the eighth grade. The U.S. Supreme Court upheld the Wisconsin Supreme Court's ruling that application of the compulsory school-attendance law to the Amish violated their rights under the Free Exercise of Religion Clause of the First Amendment (as made applicable to the states by the Fourteenth Amendment). The Court acknowledged that the case required a balancing of legitimate interests but concluded that the interest of the parents determining the religious upbringing of their children outweighed the claim of the state in its role as *parens patriae* "to extend the benefit of secondary education to children regardless of the wishes of their parents."

Mr. Chief Justice Burger delivered the opinion of the Court, which showed a commendable sensitivity to the parental interests and the ways they are threatened by secular public education: "The concept of life aloof from the world and its values is central to their faith. . . . High school attendance with teachers who are not of the Amish faith, and may even be hostile to it, interposes a serious barrier to integration of the Amish child into the Amish religious community. . . . Compulsory school attendance to the age of sixteen for Amish children carries with it a very real threat of undermining Amish community and religious practice as they exist today; they must either abandon belief and be assimilated into society at large, or be forced to migrate to some other and more tolerant region."[12]

Burger shows very little sensitivity, however, to the interests of the Amish child in choosing his own vocation in life. At one point he begs the question against anyone who suggests that some Amish children might freely and even wisely decide to enter the modern world if given the choice: "The value of all education must be assessed in terms of its capacity to prepare the child for life. It is one thing to say that compulsory education for a year or two beyond the eighth grade may be necessary when its goal is the preparation of the child for life in modern society as the majority live, but it is quite another if the goal of education be viewed as the preparation

12. *Wisconsin v. Yoder*, pp. 209, 216.

of the child for life in the separated agrarian community that is the keystone of the Amish faith."[13] But how is "the goal of education" to be viewed? That is the question that must be left open if the Court is to issue a truly neutral decision. To assume that the goal is preparation for modern commercial-industrial life is to beg the question in favor of the state, but equally, to assume that the goal is preparation for a "life aloof from the world" is to beg the question in favor of the parents. An impartial decision would assume only that education should equip the child with the knowledge and skills that will help him choose whichever sort of life best fits his native endowment and matured disposition. It should send him out into the adult world with as many open opportunities as possible, thus maximizing his chances for self-fulfillment.

More than eighty percent of the way through his opinion, the Chief Justice finally addresses the main issue: "The state's case . . . appears to rest on the potential that exemption of Amish parents from the requirements of the compulsory education law might allow some parents to act contrary to the best interests of their children by foreclosing their opportunity to make an intelligent choice between the Amish way of life and that of the outside world."[14] That is indeed the argument that Burger must rebut, and his attempt to do so is quite extraordinary:

> The same argument could, of course, be made with respect to all church schools short of college. [Burger forgets that church schools must satisfy certain minimal curricular standards if they are to be accredited by the state. The state of Wisconsin has not prohibited the Amish from establishing parochial schools that meet the same standards that other church schools do.] Indeed it seems clear that if the State is empowered, as *parens patriae*, to "save" a child from himself or his Amish parents by requiring an additional two years of compulsory formal high school education, the State will in large measure influence if not determine, the religious future of the child. Even more markedly than in *Prince*, therefore, this case involves the fundamental interest of parents, as contrasted with that of the State, to guide the religious future and education of their children.[15]

Burger seems to employ here a version of the familiar argument that to prevent one party from determining an outcome is neces-

13. *Wisconsin v. Yoder*, p. 213.
14. *Wisconsin v. Yoder*, p. 230.
15. *Wisconsin v. Yoder*, p. 230.

sarily to determine a different outcome, or to exercise undue "influence" on the final outcome. So it has been argued in similar terms that to prevent one party's coercion of a second party's decision is itself to influence that decision coercively.[16] Often this sort of argument is directed at inactions as well as actions so that the would-be guarantor of impartiality is beaten from the start. Thus it is sometimes said that to abstain from coercion is to permit an outcome that could have been prevented and thus to exercise undue influence, or (in other contexts) that not to punish is to condone. The upshot of these modes of reasoning is the conclusion that state neutrality is not merely difficult but impossible in principle, that by doing nothing, or permitting no other parties to do anything that will close a child's options before he is grown, the state in many cases itself closes some options.

There are two ways of replying to this argument of Burger's. The first is to claim that there is some reasonable conception of neutrality that is immune to his blanket dismissal, so that while there are some severe practical difficulties that stand in the way, they are not unsolvable in principle, and that in any event, even if perfect neutrality is unachievable in an imperfect world, there is hope that it can be approached or approximated to some degree. Ideally, the neutral state (in this "reasonable conception") would act to let all influences, or the largest and most random possible assortment of influences, work equally on the child, to open up all possibilities to him, without itself influencing him toward one or another of these. In that way, it can be hoped that the chief determining factor in the grown child's choice of a vocation and life-style will be his own governing values, talents, and propensities. The second reply to Burger is to ask, on the supposition that neutrality is impossible, why the Court should automatically favor the interests of the parents when they conflict with those of their children.

Despite these animadversions on Mr. Chief Justice Burger's reasoning, I do not wish to contend that the decision in *Yoder* was mis-

16. Consider also the commonly heard argument that state policies that keep religious observances and practices out of the public schools have the effect of "establishing" one religion in preference to all the others, namely the religion of "secular humanism." The conclusion then presented is not that the state should try nevertheless to be as neutral as it can, but rather that since neutrality is absolutely impossible whichever policy is adopted, the state might as well permit Christian observances.

taken. The difference between a mere eight years of elementary education and a mere ten years of mostly elementary education seems so trivial in the technologically complex modern world, that it is hard to maintain that a child who has only the former is barred from many possible careers while the child who has only the latter is not. It is plausible therefore to argue that what is gained for the educable fourteen-year-old Amish child by guaranteeing him another two years of school is more than counterbalanced by the corrosive effect on the religious bonds of the Amish community. From the philosophical standpoint, however, even the sixteen year old educable youth whose parents legally withdrew him from school has suffered an invasion of his rights-in-trust.

I am more sympathetic to the separate concurring opinion in the *Yoder* case, written by Mr. Justice White and endorsed by Justices Brennan and Stuart, than to the official majority opinion written by the Chief Justice, and I should like to underline its emphasis. These justices join the majority only because the difference between eight and ten years is minor in terms of the children's interests but possibly crucial for the very survival of the Amish sect. (Secular influences on the children had been minimal during the first eight years since they attended a "nearby rural schoolhouse," with an overwhelming proportion of students of the Amish faith, none of whom played rock records, watched television, or the like.) Nevertheless, even though the facts of this case are not favorable for the State's position, the case is still a close one, and had the facts been somewhat different, these justices would have upheld the C–rights represented by the state whatever the cost to the Amish sect. "This would be a very different case for me," Mr. Justice White wrote, "if respondents' claim were that their religion forbade their children from attending any school at any time and from complying in any way with the educational standards set by the State."[17] In that hypothetical case, as in various intermediate ones where we can imagine that the respondents withdrew their children after two or four years of schooling, no amount of harm to the parents' interest in the religious upbringing of their children could overturn the children's right to an open future.

White eloquently answers Burger's claim that compulsory education of Amish youth in large modern high schools is in effect a

17. *Wisconsin v. Yoder*, p. 236.

kind of indoctrination in secular values. Education can be compulsory, he argues, only because, or only when, it is neutral:

> . . . the State is not concerned with the maintenance of an educational system as an end in itself; it is rather attempting to nurture and develop the human potential of its children, whether Amish or non-Amish; to expand their knowledge, broaden their sensibilities, kindle their imagination, foster a spirit of free inquiry, and increase their human understanding and tolerance. It is possible that most Amish children will wish to continue living the rural life of their parents, in which case their training at home will adequately equip them for their future role. Others, however, may wish to become nuclear physicists, ballet dancers, computer programmers, or historians, and for these occupations, formal training will be necessary. . . . A State has a legitimate interest not only in seeking to develop the latent talents of its children but also in seeking to prepare them for the life style that they may later choose, or at least to provide them with an option other than the life they have led in the past.[18]

The corrective emphasis of the White concurring opinion then is on the danger of using *Yoder* uncritically as a precedent for finding against children's *C*–rights when they are clearly in conflict with the supervisory rights of their parents. A quite different case, involving a child custody decision, will illustrate the equal and opposite danger of overruling parental rights for the suppositious future interests of a child interpreted in a flagrantly non-neutral manner. This horror story is an example of a court taking far too seriously its right under *parens patriae* by enforcing on a child its own special and partisan conception of the way of life that is truly best for it. I refer to the case of six year old Mark Painter of Ames, Iowa.[19] An automobile accident took the lives of his mother and sister. His father then left him temporarily with his prosperous maternal grandparents on a large Iowa farm, and went to a suburb of San Francisco to begin a new career. A year later, having remarried, he went back to Iowa to pick up his son and return with him to his

18. *Wisconsin v. Yoder*, pp. 237–38.
19. See the book about the case by his father: Hal Painter, *Mark, I Love You* (New York: Simon & Schuster, 1968). The citations in notes 19 and 20 below are from Justice William C. Stuart's decision in the Iowa Supreme Court, reprinted as an Appendix in the paperback edition of *Mark, I Love You* (New York: Ballantine, 1969).

new home. The grandparents refused to give up the boy, however, and the case went to court. A lower court decision returning the boy to the custody of his natural father was eventually overturned by a state Supreme Court decision favoring the grandparents. The U.S. Supreme Court refused to review that decision, and thus a father was legally deprived of the custody of his own son.

The opinion of the Iowa Supreme Court is a melancholy document. Mr. Painter's new home, it concluded, would not satisfy the child's right to well-rounded growth into full maturity: "Our conclusion as to the type of home Mr. Painter would offer is based upon his Bohemian approach to finances and life in general. . . . He is either an agnostic or an atheist and has no concern for formal religious training. . . . He has read a lot of Zen Buddhism. . . . Mrs. Painter is Roman Catholic. . . . He is a political liberal and got into difficulty in a job at the University of Washington for his support of the activities of the American Civil Liberties Union. . . . We believe the Painter household would be unstable, unconventional, arty, Bohemian, and probably intellectually stimulating."[20] The home of Mark's Protestant Sunday-school-teaching grandparents, on the other hand, was spacious and commodious, and sure to provide him "with a stable, dependable, conventional, middle-class, Middle West background."[21]

If a parent, as such, has a legally recognized right to the custody of his own child (and surely this must be the case) then we should expect courts to infringe that right only with the greatest reluctance and only for the most compelling reasons. One such reason would be conflict with an even more important right of the child himself. Parents who beat, torture, or multilate their children, or who willfully refuse to permit them to be educated, can expect the state as *parens patriae* to intervene and assign the children to the custody of court-appointed trustees. Given satisfaction of reasonable moral standards of care and education, however, no court has the right to impose its own conception of the good life on a child over its natural parents' objections. The state cannot properly select the best influences for a child; it can only insist that all public influences be kept open, that all children through accredited schools become acquainted with a great variety of facts and diversified ac-

20. Painter, *Mark, I Love You*, pp. 226–27.
21. Painter, *Mark, I Love You*, p. 225.

counts and evaluations of the myriad human arrangements in the world and in history. This is what it means for parents to "take their chances" with external influences. But apart from that, every parent is free to provide any kind of religious upbringing he chooses, or none at all; to send his child to public or accredited private schools, sectarian or non-sectarian; to attempt to transmit his own ideals, moral and political, whatever they may be, to his child; in short, to create whatever environment of influence he can for his child, subject to the state's important but minimal standards of humanity, health, and education. For a child to be exposed mainly and directly to unconventional values is still, after all, a long way from "martyrdom."

As to the content of the values of any particular parents, there the liberal state is and must be neutral. Indeed, the state must be as neutral between atheism and theism in the private household of citizens as it is between Protestantism and Catholicism. The wretched decision in the Painter case, therefore, can be construed in part as a violation of a citizen's right to the free "non-exercise" of religion, for reasons that include no weighable interest or right of his child. It sounds innocuous enough to say that a child's welfare has priority even over a parent's right of custody; but this is no more than an empty platitude when the child's welfare is not objectively and unarguably at issue.

PHILOSOPHICAL ISSUES OF CONFLICTING RIGHTS

Paternalism

The coherence of the above account of the child's right to an open future is threatened by a number of philosophical riddles. The existence of such a right, as we have seen, sets limits to the ways in which parents may raise their own children, and even imposes duties on the state, in its role as *parens patriae,* to enforce those limits. The full statement of the grounds for these protective duties will invoke the interrelated ideals of autonomy (or self-determination) and self-fulfillment, and these concepts are notoriously likely to generate philosophical confusion. Moreover, both friends and enemies of the child's right to an open future are likely to use the obscure and emotionally charged epithet "paternalism," the one side accusingly, the other apologetically, a practice that can only detract further from conceptual clarity.

The pejorative term "paternalism" is commonly applied to acts of authorities or rule-makers, which are thought to treat adults as if they were children: for example, orders prohibiting some sort of predominately self-regarding behavior, when they are issued for the subject's "own good" quite apart from his own considered preferences in the matter, or actions that deliberately impose some pattern on the subject's life without his consent or even against his wishes, but once more, like bitter medicine, "for his own good." How is it possible then for parents to be "paternalistic" in a similarly derogatory sense toward their own children? The term can be applied pejoratively in this way only because there is a series of stages in a child's growth between total helplessness and incapacity at the beginning and near self-sufficiency at the threshold of adulthood. Blameable paternalism must consist in treating the child at a given stage as if he were at some earlier, less developed stage. But paternalism in the upbringing of children, in some sense, is inevitable and therefore wholly proper, whether imposed by the state in the child's interest or by the parents themselves, for there will be some respects at least in which even an older child cannot know his own interest, some respects in which he must be protected from his own immature and uninformed judgment. Moreover, since children are not born with a precisely determined character structure, they must be socialized by measures of discipline if they are to become fit members of the adult community, and this must be done even if it is against the wishes of the presocialized children themselves. As Kenneth Henley puts it: "We cannot always await their consent to the sometimes painful steps of growing up."[22]

It is characteristic of parents, of course, not only to protect children from their own folly, but also to protect them from external dangers generally, including the dangers posed by other persons. This is a task in which the state joins as a cooperative partner defining crimes against children and enforcing criminal laws by its police powers and the threat of punishment. Since the state shares this safeguarding function with willing parents, its protective policies are paternalistic in an innocent, non-pejorative sense, namely that of "protective in a manner characteristic of parents." In the

22. Kenneth Henley, "The Authority to Educate" in *Having Children: Philosophical and Legal Reflections on Parenthood*, ed. by Onora O'Neill and William Ruddick (New York: Oxford Univ. Pr., 1979), p. 255. Henley's excellent article is strongly recommended.

cases we have considered in this essay, however, the state exercises its tutelary powers for the sake of children against their own parents. These state policies are paternalistic in the general sense of "characteristically parental," but the question of their justification in all but extreme cases is genuinely controversial. Insofar as paternalism has acquired a fixed derogatory overtone, it can be applied to these difficult cases only at the risk of equivocation between pejorative and neutral senses and consequent question-begging against the defender of state intervention.

Autonomy

Typically the state must shoulder a greater burden of justification for its interferences with parents for the sake of their children than that which is borne by parents in justification of their interferences with children for the children's own sake. That is because state action by its very nature tends to be cumbersome and heavy-handed, and because it constitutes a threat to such well-established parental rights as the right to supervise the upbringing of one's own children and the right to the free exercise of one's own religion (which unavoidably influences the developing attitudes and convictions of the children). But although the burden on the state is characteristically heavier than that shouldered by parents for their own interventions, it is essentially of the same general kind, requiring the same sorts of reasons. In either case, the justification appeals (to speak roughly at first) to the eventual autonomy and to the good of the child.

The word "autonomy," which plays such an essential role in the discussion of children's rights, has at least two relevant senses. It can refer either to the capacity to govern oneself, which of course is a matter of degree, or (on the analogy to a political state) to the sovereign authority to govern oneself, which is absolute within one's own moral boundaries (one's "territory," "realm," "sphere," or "business"). Note that there are two parallel senses of the term "independent," the first of which refers to self-sufficiency, the *de facto* capacity to support oneself, direct one's own life, and be finally responsible for one's own decisions; the second, applied mainly to political states, refers to *de jure* sovereignty and the rights of self-determination. In a nutshell, one sense of autonomy (and also of independence) refers to the capacity and the other to the right of self-determination. When the state justifies its interference with parental liberty by reference to the eventual autonomy of the protected child, it argues that the mature adult that the child will become, like all free citizens, has a right of self-determination, and that that right is violated in advance if certain crucial and irrevocable decisions determining the course of his life are made by anyone else before he has the capacity of self-determination himself.

One standard way of deriving the right of self-determination is to base it solidly on the good of self-fulfillment.[23] A given normal adult is much more likely to know his own interests, talents, and natural dispositions (the stuff of which his good is composed) than is any other party, and much more capable therefore of directing his own affairs to the end of his own good than is a government official or a parent at an earlier stage who might preempt his choices for him. The individual's advantages in this regard are so great that for all practical purposes we can hold that recognition and enforcement of the right of self-determination (autonomy) is a causally necessary condition for the achievement of self-fulfillment (the individual's own good). This is the view of John Stuart Mill, who argued in *On Liberty* that the attempt even of a genuinely benevolent state to impose upon an adult an external conception of his own good is almost certain to be self-defeating, and that an adult's own good is "best provided for by allowing him to take his own means of pursuing it"[24] Promotion of human well-being and the prevention of harms are primary in Mill's system, so that even so basic a right as that of self-determination must be derived from its conducibility to them. In those rare cases where we can know that free exercise of a person's autonomy will be against his own interests, as, for example, when he freely negotiates his own slavery in exchange for some other good, we are justified in interfering with his liberty in order to protect him from harm.

The second standard interpretation of the right of self-determination holds that it is entirely underivative, as morally basic as the good of self-fulfillment itself. There is no necessity, in this view,

23. For a further analysis of self-fulfillment, see my "Absurd Self-fulfillment: An Essay on the Merciful Perversity of the Gods," in *Time and Cause, Essays Presented to Richard Taylor*, edited by Peter van Inwagen (Dortrecht, The Netherlands: Reidel, 1979), pp. 255–81.

24. John Stuart Mill, *On Liberty*, chap. 5, para. 11.

that free exercise of a person's autonomy will promote his own
good, but even where self-determination is likely, on objective evidence, to lead to the person's own harm, others do not have a right
to intervene coercively "for his own good." By and large, a person
will be better able to achieve his own good by making his own decisions, but even where the opposite is true, others may not intervene, for autonomy is even more important a thing than personal
well-being. The life that a person threatens by his own rashness is
after all *his* life. For that reason alone, he must be the one to decide—for better or worse—what is to be done with it in that private
realm where the interests of others are not directly involved.[25]

A compromise way of regarding the adult's right of autonomy
is to think of it as neither derivative from nor more basic than its
possessor's own good (self-fulfillment), but rather as coordinate
with it. In the more plausible versions of this third view, a person's
own good, in the vast majority of cases will be most reliably fur-
thered if he is allowed to make his own choices in self-regarding
matters, but where that coincidence of values does not hold, one
must simply do one's best to balance autonomy against personal
well-being, and decide between them intuitively, since neither has
automatic priority over the other.[26] In any case, the two distinct
ideals of sovereign autonomy (self-determination) and personal
well-being (self-fulfillment) are both likely to enter, indeed to
dominate, the discussion of the grounding of the child's right to an
open future. That right (or class of rights) must be held in trust
either out of respect for the sovereign independence of the emerg-
ing adult (and derivatively in large part for his own good), or for
the sake of the lifelong well-being of the person who is still a child
(a well-being from which the need of self-government "by and
large" can be derived), or from both. In such ways the good (self-
fulfillment) and the right (self-determination) of the child enter
the justificatory discussion. And both can breed paradox from the
start, unless handled with care.

25. This second interpretation of autonomy rights is defended in my
essay "Legal Paternalism," *Canadian Journal of Philosophy* 1 (1971): 105–
24, and also in my "Freedom and Behavioral Control" in *The Encyclopedia
of Bioethics*, edited by Warren T. Reich (New York: The Free Press, 1978),
vol. 1, pp. 93–101.
26. See for example Jonathan Glover, *Causing Death and Saving Lives*
(New York: Penguin, 1977), pp. 74–85.

Paradoxes of self-determination

The paradoxes I have in mind both have the form, prima facie, of vicious circles. Consider first the self-determination circle. If we have any coherent conception of the fully self-determined adult, he is a person who has determined both his own life-circumstances and his own character. The former consists of his career-type (doctor, lawyer, merchant, chief), his life-style (swinger, hermit, jogger, scholar), and his religious affiliation and attitude (piety, hypocrisy, indifference, total absorption), among other things. The latter is that set of habitual traits that we create by our own actions and cultivated feelings in given types of circumstances, our characteristic habits of response to life's basic kinds of situations. Aristotle analyzed these as deeply rooted dispositions to act or feel in certain ways in certain kinds of circumstances, and since his time it has become a philosophical truism that we are, in large part, the products of our own making, since each time we act or feel in a given way in a given kind of circumstance, we strengthen the disposition to act or feel in that way (brave or cowardly, kind or cruel, warm or cold) in similar circumstances in the future. Now, whatever policy is adopted by a child's parents, and whatever laws are passed and enforced by the state, the child's options in respect to his life's circumstances and character will be substantially narrowed well before he is an adult. He will have to be socialized and educated, and these processes will inevitably influence the development of his own values, tastes, and standards, which will, in turn, determine in part how he acts, feels, and chooses. That, in turn, will reinforce his tendencies to act, feel, and choose in similar ways in the future, until his character is set. If the parents and the state try to evade the responsibility for character and career formation by an early policy of drift, that will have consequences on the child too, for which they shall have to answer. And in any case, simply by living their own lives as they choose, the parents will be forming an environment around the child that will tend to shape his budding loyalties and habits, and they will be providing in their own selves ready models for emulation.[27] This inevitable narrow-

27. Henley makes this point especially well in his discussion of the parents' religious rights: "In the early years of the child's socialization, he will be surrounded by the religious life of his parents; since the parents have a right to live such religious lives, and on the assumption that children will

ing of options can yet be done without violation of the child's *C*–
right of self-determination provided it is somehow in accordance
with the child's actual or presumptive, explicit or tacit consent.
But we can hardly ask the child's actual explicit consent to our for-
mative decisions because at the point when these processes start—
where the twig begins to be bent—he is not developed enough to
give his consent. But neither has he values and preferences of his
own for the parents to consult and treat as clues to what his disposition to give or withhold consent would be. At the early stage
the parents cannot even ask in any helpful way what the child will
be like, apart from the parental policies under consideration, when
he finally does have relevant preferences, values, and the capacity
to consent. That outcome will depend on the character the child
will have then, which in part depends, in turn, on how his parents
raise him now. They are now shaping the person who is to decide
later and whose presumptive later decision cannot be divined. As
Henley remarks: "Whether a certain sort of life would please a
child often depends upon how he has been socialized, and so we
cannot decide to socialize him for that life by asking whether that
kind of life would please him."[28]

The paradox of self-determination can be put even more forcefully as an infinite regress. If the grown-up offspring is to determine his own life, and be at least in large part the product of his
own self-determination, he must already have a self fully formed
and capable of doing the determining. But he cannot very well have
determined *that* self on his own, because he would have to have
been already a formed self to do that, and so on, ad infinitum. The
vicious circle is avoided only by positing an infinite series of prior
selves, each the product on an earlier self.[29]

---

normally be raised by their parents, parental influence on the child's religious
life is both legitimate and unavoidable. But at such an early stage it can
hardly be said that coercion is involved; the child simply lives in the midst
of a religious way of life and comes to share in it. But surely the assertion that
the child is born with religious liberty must entail that parents are under at
least moral constraints not to *force* their religious beliefs upon the child once
he is capable of forming his own views. . . ." "The Authority to Educate,"
pp. 260–61.

28. Henley, "The Authority to Educate," p. 256.
29. Cf. John Wisdom's not altogether playful argument that moral re-

Paradoxes of self-fulfillment

The paradoxes of self-fulfillment present much the same sort of appearance as the paradoxes of self-determination and can be expressed in quite parallel language. These arise, however, not when we ask what a child will come to prefer, choose, or consent to later in the exercise of his matured autonomy, but rather, simply, when we ask what would be good for him, his presumptive choice notwithstanding. To answer this question we must seek to learn his governing propensities, his skills and aptitudes, his highest potential. We must gauge how his nature is "wound up" and in what direction he is faced, in order to determine what would fulfill his most basic tendencies. We stumble into the vicious circle when we note that if a person's own good is to be understood as self-fulfillment, we cannot fully know the small child's long term future good until the child's "nature" is fully formed, but equally we cannot determine how best to shape his nature until we know what will be for his own good. We cannot just leave the child's entire future open for him to decide later according to his settled adult values, because he must and will begin to acquire those values now in childhood, whatever we do. In closing his future options in some ways now by our educating, by our socializing, by our choice of influential environments, we cannot be guided entirely by what accords with the child's own future character, because that character will in large part be a product of the self we are molding now. In a nutshell: the parents help create some of the interests whose fulfillment will constitute the child's own good. They cannot aim at an independent conception of the child's own good in deciding how to do this, because to some extent the child's own good (self-fulfillment) depends on which interests the parents decide to create. The circle is thus closed.

RESOLUTION OF THE PARADOXES

Closed, but not closed tight. The plausible-sounding propositions that seem to lock us into paradox in reality are only approximate generalizations, merely partial truths whose soft spots make pos-

---

sponsibility presupposes that we have *always* existed, in his *Problems of Mind and Matter* (Cambridge: Cambridge Univ. Pr., 1934), pp. 110–34.

sible escape-hatches. The paradoxes stem from a failure to appreciate how various judgments used in their formulation are only partly
true, and how certain central distinctions are matters of degree. It is
an overstatement, for example, that there is any early stage at which
a child's character is wholly unformed and his talents and temperament entirely plastic, without latent bias or limit, and another that
there can be no self-determination unless the self that does the determining is already fully formed. Moreover, it is a distortion to
represent the distinction between child and adult in the rigid manner presupposed by the paradoxes.

There is no sharp line between the two stages of human life; they
are really only useful abstractions from a continuous process of development every phase of which differs only in degree from that
preceding it. Many or most of a child's C–rights-in-trust have already become A-rights by the time he is ten or twelve. Any "mere
child" beyond the stage of infancy is only a child in some respects,
and already an adult in others. Such dividing lines as the eighteenth
or twenty-first birthday are simply approximations (plausible
guesses) for the point where all the natural rights-in-trust have become actual A-rights. In the continuous development of the relative-
adult out of the relative-child there is no point before which the
child himself has no part in his own shaping, and after which he is
the sole responsible maker of his own character and life plan. The
extent of the child's role in his own shaping is again a process of
constant and continuous growth already begun at birth, as indeed
is the "size" of his self, that is, the degree to which it is already
formed and fixed.

Right from the beginning the newborn infant has a kind of rudi-
mentary character consisting of temperamental proclivities and a
genetically fixed potential for the acquisition of various talents and
skills. The standard sort of loving upbringing and a human social
environment in the earliest years will be like water added to de-
hydrated food, filling it out and actualizing its stored-in tendencies.
Then the child's earliest models for imitation will make an ineluc-
table mark on him. He will learn one language rather than another,
for instance, and learn it with a particular accent and inflection. His
own adult linguistic style will be in the making virtually from the
beginning. For the first year or two he will have no settled dispositions of action and feeling of the kind Aristotle called virtues and
vices (excellences and defects of character), but as Aristotle said,

he is born with the capacity to acquire such dispositions, and the process is underway very early as his basic habits of response are formed and reinforced.

At a time so early that the questions of how to socialize and educate the child have not even arisen yet, the twig will be bent in a certain definite direction. From then on, in promoting the child's eventual autonomy and well-being the parents will have to respect that initial bias from heredity and early environment. Thus from the beginning the child must—inevitably *will*—have some input in its own shaping, the extent of which will grow continuously even as the child's character itself does. I think that we can avoid or at least weaken the paradoxes if we remember that the child can contribute towards the making of his own self and circumstances in ever-increasing degree. Always the self that contributes to the making of the new self is itself the product both of outside influences and an earlier self that was not quite as fully formed. That earlier self, in turn, was the product both of outside influences and a still earlier self that was still less fully formed and fixed, and so on, all the way back to infancy. At every subsequent stage the immature child plays an ever-greater role in the creation of his own life, until at the arbitrarily fixed point of full maturity or adulthood, he is at last fully and properly in charge of himself, sovereign within his terrain, his more or less finished character the product of a complicated interaction of external influences and ever-increasing contributions from his own earlier self. At least that is how growth proceeds when parents and other authorities raise a child with maximum regard for the autonomy of the adult he will one day be. That is the most sense that we can make of the ideal of the "self-made person," but it is an intelligible idea, I think, with no paradox in it.

Similarly, the parents who raise their child in such a way as to promote his self-fulfillment most effectively will at every stage try to strengthen the basic tendencies of the child as manifested at that stage. They will give him opportunities to develop his strongest talents, for instance, after having enjoyed opportunities to discover by various experiments just what those talents are. And they will steer the child toward the type of career that requires the kind of temperament the child already has rather than a temperament that is alien to him by his very nature. There can be no self-fulfillment for a child prone to sedentary activity by his native body type and endowed with fine motor control over his sensitive fingers if he is inescapably led into a job calling for a large-muscled, energetic person with high gross motor control but no patience for small painstaking tasks, or vice-versa. The child will even have very basic tendencies toward various kinds of attitudes from an early stage, at least insofar as they grow naturally out of his inherited temperamental propensities. He may be the naturally gregarious, outgoing sort, or the kind of person who will naturally come to treasure his privacy and to keep his own counsels; he may appreciate order and structure more or less than spontaneity and freedom; he may be inclined, *ceteris paribus*, to respect or to challenge authority. Such attitudes grow from basic depositions of temperament and are the germ, in turn, of fundamental convictions and styles of life that the child will still be working out and trying to understand and justify when he is an adult. The discerning parent will see all of these things ever more clearly as the child grows older, and insofar as he steers the child at all, it will be in the child's own preferred directions. At the very least he will not try to turn him upstream and make him struggle against his own deepest currents. Then if the child's future is left open as much as possible for his own finished self to determine, the fortunate adult that emerges will already have achieved, without paradox, a certain amount of self-fulfillment, a consequence in large part of his own already autonomous choices in promotion of his own natural preferences.

VI

Medical Paternalism, Voluntariness, and Comprehension

Tom L. Beauchamp

PATERNALISM SEEMS TO PERVADE MODERN SOCIETY, for many actions, rules, and laws are commonly justified by appeal to a paternalistic principle. Examples in medicine include court orders for blood transfusions when patients have refused them, involuntary commitment to institutions for treatment, intervention to stop "rational" suicides, resuscitating patients who have asked not to be resuscitated, withholding medical information requested by patients, denial of an innovative therapy to someone who wishes to try it, and some government efforts to promote health. Other health-related examples include laws requiring motorcyclists to wear helmets and motorists to wear seat belts and the regulations of governmental agencies such as the Food and Drug Administration banning the purchase of possibly harmful or inefficacious drugs and chemicals. In all cases the motivation is the beneficent promotion of health and welfare. Beneficence is an acceptable moral principle, but not everything flowing from beneficent motives is commendable; and limiting the liberty of the beneficiaries is often flatly unwelcome because of the apparent invasion of autonomy. Paternalism is the issue generated by this conflict of principles.

In the case of medical paternalism, it is often said that the patient/physician relationship is essentially paternalistic. This view is held because patients can be so ill that their judgments or voluntary abilities are significantly affected, or they may be incapable of grasping important information about their case, thus leaving them in no position to reach carefully reasoned decisions about their medical treatment. Illness, injury, depression, fear, the threat of death, and traditional staples of the medical profession such as drugs may overwhelm patients, rendering them doubtfully able to ascertain their own best interests. Moreover, every increase in illness, ignorance, and quantity of medication can increase the patient's dependence on his or her physician; and too, physicians constantly encourage patients with small lies intended to raise their spirits, when in fact matters are either hopeless or beyond the physician's capacities. Hospitals and the medical profession thus seem committed to a paternalistic orientation. Some recent writers not only support this paternalistic relationship but have even argued that deference to patient autonomy or to requirements of informed consent are dangerous to a patient's health and can lead to questionable clinical practices that compromise sound medical judgment.[1]

On the other hand, the paternalism of the medical profession has been under attack in recent years, especially by defenders of patient autonomy. They hold that physicians intervene too often and assume too much control over their patients' choices. Recent philosophical, legal, and medical articles and books have often reflected this harsh judgment of the profession. Philosophers and lawyers have tended to support the view that patient autonomy is the decisive factor in the patient/physician relationship and that intervention can be valid only when persons are substantially nonvoluntary. Physicians too have increasingly criticized authoritarianism in their profession. The latter concern resulted in a recent draft of ethical principles by the American Medical Association which asserts that "paternalism by the profession is no longer appropriate."[2] It seems timely, then, to reflect on the nature of paternalism and the extent to which it is or is not justified.

THE DEFINITION OF PATERNALISM

Traditionally, the word "paternalism" has been loosely used to refer to practices of treating individuals in the way a father treats

1. Elizabeth F. Loftus and James F. Friess, "Informed Consent may be Hazardous to your Health," *Science* April 6, 1979, p. 11; R. L. Katz, "Informed Consent: Is It Bad Medicine?" *Western Journal of Medicine* 126 (1977): 426–28; B. M. Patten and W. Stump, "Death Related to Informed Consent," *Texas Medicine* 74 (1978): 49–50.

2. As quoted in Robert M. Veatch and Ernest Tai, "Talking About Death: Patterns of Lay and Professional Change," *The Annals of the American Academy of Political and Social Science*, 447 (Jan., 1980): 38.

his children. When this analogy is applied to medical professionals, two features of the paternal role are assumed: the father's beneficence, that is, that the father holds the interests of his children paramount; and the father's authority, that is, that he makes certain decisions for his children and controls certain affairs rather than letting them make the decisions or take control. The word "paternalism" is used more formally in moral philosophy to refer to practices that restrict the liberty of individuals without their consent. The justification for such actions is either the prevention of some harm they may do to themselves or the production of some good for them that they would not otherwise secure for themselves.

H. L. A. Hart has defined paternalism as "the protection of people against themselves."[3] This loose definition is unsuitable, however, for it seems misleadingly to include laws or acts designed to protect individuals against quite unintended results of their thoughts or actions, such as drinking polluted water in mountain streams. Gerald Dworkin has provided a more careful, but still inadequate definition: paternalism is "the interference with a person's liberty of action justified by reasons referring exclusively to the welfare, good, happiness, needs, interests or values of the person being coerced."[4] Allen Buchanan has suggested that this characterization be revised to include "interference with a person's freedom of action or freedom of information, or the deliberate dissemination of misinformation."[5] This is an important and acceptable addition, especially for discussions of informed consent, because withholding of information that consequently limits a person's liberty is paternalistic. A battery action can be brought in law, for example, for a violation of liberty (self-determination) merely on grounds that relevant information was withheld. Of course, disclosure itself could be paternalistic if a person had asked not to receive information, but Buchanan's addition is valuable when construed to require any actual restriction of liberty.

The reasons for restricting liberty or for overriding autonomy mentioned by Dworkin are important. Hart's definition makes no attempt to give justifying reasons for the "protection of people

3. H. L. A. Hart, *Law, Liberty, and Morality* (Stanford: Stanford Univ. Pr., 1963), p. 31.
4. Gerald Dworkin, "Paternalism," *Monist* 56 (1972): 65.
5. Allen Buchanan, "Medical Paternalism," *Philosophy and Public Affairs* 7 (1978): 371–72.

against themselves," whereas Dworkin cites standard reasons of beneficence (or nonmaleficence) as justifications for interference with liberty. In cases where a refusal of treatment is overridden and a person is detained in the hospital, the detention would be paternalistic in Dworkin's sense, because it limits the person's freedom of choice and is performed for his or her own good rather than for the good of others.

Although it is common to define paternalistic intervention as coercive (see Dworkin's final word), it is best to require only that there be a limitation of liberty. Coercion is exceedingly difficult to define, and there are numerous apparently noncoercive means of limiting both internal and external voluntariness. Powerful incentives, restricted supplies, high taxation rates, and withholding information, for example, may limit liberty without being coercive (though paternalistic interventions may of course be coercive). One objection to this common way of analyzing the moral problem of paternalism as a liberty-limiting principle is that it violates older common sense and legal concepts of paternalism. The *parens patriae* powers of the state, for example, are invoked in the courts when dealing with cases of incompetents who have no capacity for liberty of thought or action. In *Canterbury v. Spence*[6] and *Superintendent of Belchertown State School v. Saikewicz*, both courts speak of "paternalistic actions" and *parens patriae* powers. In *Saikewicz* the court invokes the legal doctrine of *parens patriae* in discussing what the state must do to "protect the 'best interests' of the incompetent person."[7] If this intervention were taken to express paternalism in morals as well as law, then there obviously would be no question of limiting liberty or autonomy. But this usage would confuse paternalism with wardship (an unsurprising conflation in a legal context). Similarly, even so arch an antipaternalist as Thomas Szasz links paternalistic justifications for involuntary commitment to justification for the "coercive" control of children and the mentally retarded.[8] Ordinary language also allows paternalism to apply to legally incompetent children and even to infants. It is tempting, then,

---

6. *Canterbury v. Spence*, 464 F. 2d 772 (D.C. Cir. 1972).

7. *Superintendent of Belchertown v. Saikewicz*, 373 Mass. 728, 370 N.E. 2d 417 at 427 (1977). Italics added.

8. "Involuntary Mental Hospitalization ...," in Tom L. Beauchamp and Leroy Walters, eds., *Contemporary Issues in Bioethics* (Belmont, Ca.: Dickenson, 1978), p. 556.

to follow law and common usage by distinguishing paternalistic treatment of competents and paternalistic treatment of incompetents, but allowing both to be forms of paternalism.

There are, however, several reasons for resisting this temptation. First, the moral issue of paternalism is ubiquitously drawn in the literature as an issue of freedom. To move the problem to the level of those who have no capacity for liberty would be merely to broaden the term in a way that detracts from the central moral issue (liberty-limitation or violations of autonomy), while at the same time changing the meaning of the term as it is used in the key literature on the subject. Second, the concept of "*parens patriae* powers" has its own subtleties and complexities. The courts do not apply this notion across the same range of thought and conduct envisaged as paternalistic in philosophical literature, and to incorporate this legal doctrine would in the end prove more confusing than helpful. It is better here to keep the legal and the moral problems separate, and paternalism is clearly a moral problem. Third, many interventions with incompetents are noncontroversially justified, and if there were a form of "incompetence paternalism," there would obviously be no antipaternalists. But, as we shall now see, there is long history of antipaternalism.

I shall therefore not depart from the standard ways of analyzing the concept of paternalism in terms of liberty-limitation. Any moral principle that is paternalistic must state that limiting a person's liberty is justified if through his or her own thoughts, responses, or actions some self-harm would be produced or an important self-good would fail to be secured. In passing I note that there are other liberty-limiting principles besides the paternalistic principle. These include, for example, the offense principle (the restriction of conduct because it is offensive to others) and the welfare principle (the limitation of one person's liberty in order to benefit another). However, the single most important liberty-limiting principle for purposes of contrast with the paternalistic principle is the harm principle. This principle states that when specific kinds of harm are caused to a person or a group by another person or group, it is justifiable to limit the liberty of those who inflict the harm for the purpose of protecting those being harmed. The paternalistic principle applies in cases of harm only if the harm is caused by an individual to himself or herself; the harm principle applies only if the harm is caused to one party by another. These distinctions, and indeed much of the entire controversy about paternalism, have their origins in the moral theory of John Stuart Mill, as we shall now see.

PATERNALISM AND ANTIPATERNALISM

On Liberty (1859) is the classic source of antipaternalism. Mill attempts in this work to delineate the proper limits of social control over the individual by arguing that the harm principle alone is a valid principle of social control over individual liberty, whether such control is legal, religious, economic, or of some other type.[9] He defends his view with the utilitarian argument that exclusive use of this principle, however dangerous to prevailing social beliefs, would produce the best possible conditions for social progress and for developing individual talent. He further argues that society is improved by tolerating all forms of liberty that produce no harm to others, instead of "compelling each to live as seems good to the rest." He notes, however, that certain actions which may be exclusively "self-harming" when performed in private may constitute a harm or offense against others when performed in public. While both paternalism and Mill's harm principle arguably rest on considerations of beneficence, any paternalistic principle, no matter how moderately formulated, must be condemned in a system which recognizes only the harm principle as valid.

Arguments favorable to paternalism

Supposedly it is for paternalistic reasons that we think persons should not be allowed to sell themselves into slavery, barter themselves to a doctor for dangerous experiments, or take morphine purely for the sake of pleasure. These are uncommon occurrences in most ages and times, but the believer in paternalism is not deterred by the rarity of these occasions. Similarly in medicine, it might be argued, paternalistic interventions are generally unwarranted, but there are occasions when the physician quite validly intervenes. The ultimate philosophical commitments of those who defend this position on paternalism vary, but they often proceed by citing practices most all of us would agree are justified and which presumably spring from paternalistic motives. Interventions to pre-

9. John Stuart Mill, *On Liberty*, ed. Gertrude Himmelfarb (New York: Penquin, 1974), pp. 68–69.

vent suicide by a depressed patient, lying to a stroke victim in precarious circumstances, and overriding a refusal of critical chemotherapy by a mentally ill patient are cases that limited paternalists view as justified interventions or nondisclosures. It is then assumed that if the conditions justifying these paternalistically motivated practices can be delineated, these conditions must be independent of the harm principle, and therefore paternalism has been justified and antipaternalism refuted.

"The paternalistic principle" is actually an umbrella term covering numerous principles, for many mutually exclusive views have been defended as appropriate forms of paternalism. The belief that paternalism is justified is usually defended in either a broad form, which may be called *extensive* paternalism, or a narrow form, which may be called *limited* paternalism. H. L. A. Hart's general characterization of an extensive paternalism is representative: "Paternalism—the protection of people against themselves—is a perfectly coherent policy. . . . No doubt if we no longer sympathise with [Mill's] criticism this is due, in part, to a general decline in the belief that individuals know their own interests best, and to an increased awareness of a great range of factors which diminish the significance to be attached to an apparently free choice or to consent."[10] Hart implies that because we now appreciate the factors inhibiting a voluntary and informed consent, paternalism is a "perfectly coherent policy." This thesis obviously could be formulated to have an extensive application in public health and medicine. In most recent formulations of the proper scope of extensive paternalism it has been said that individuals or the state may limit a person's liberty if the person is protected against his or her own actions, where those actions are unreasonably risky (for example, being a subject of high-risk medical experimentation), are generally not in the person's own best interest when his best interest is knowable by others (as some believe in the case of suicide), or are potentially dangerous and irreversible in effect (as some drugs are).

Limited paternalism contrasts sharply with extensive paternalism. Paternalism is justified, according to limited paternalists, only in rather extreme and uncommon circumstances. Because paternalism is a liberty-limiting or autonomy-limiting principle, its use necessarily violates a moral principle against invading the freedom of an-

10. H. L. A. Hart, *Law, Liberty, and Morality*, pp. 31–33.

other. Therefore, any justification of such actions must be strong enough to outweigh the "evil" of this invasion of liberty. According to this general position, paternalism is justified only if: (1) the harms or violations prevented from occurring to the person or the benefits produced are greater than those (if any) caused by the interference with the person's liberty; and (2) it is universally justified under relevantly similar circumstances always to treat persons in this way.[11] Many but not all writers add a third condition requiring that the person's liberty is already restricted by some condition seriously encumbering autonomy; that is, the person must be substantially nonvoluntary in the circumstances .(This last condition will obviously not be held to be a necessary condition of justified paternalism if one believes that some moral principle(s) can override the principle of autonomy in the case of purely self-regarding conduct independent of considerations of the person's voluntariness.)

Dworkin and John Rawls have argued that a cautious paternalism should be regarded as a form of "social insurance policy" that fully rational persons would take out in order to protect themselves. As Rawls puts it, such persons "will want to insure themselves against the possibility that their powers are undeveloped and they cannot rationally advance their interests, as in the case of children."[12] Such persons would know, for example, that they might be tempted at times to make decisions that are potentially dangerous and irreversible. They might at other times encounter social pressures to do something they honestly believe too risky, such as the social pressure involved in accepting a challenge to fight for one's honor. In still other cases persons might not sufficiently understand or appreciate dangers that are relevant to their conduct or might seriously underestimate probable outcomes; for example, one might not appreciate the facts about research on smoking even after hearing extensive public health information on the subject. Instead of informing persons of the facts, or teaching them to appreciate the facts, which may not always be possible, Rawls and Dworkin conclude that a rational agent would agree to a limited grant of power to others for paternalistic interventions and would even "consent

11. See, e.g., Bernard M. Gert and Charles Culver, "Paternalistic Behavior," *Philosophy and Public Affairs* 6 (1976): 45–57.

12. John Rawls, *A Theory of Justice* (Cambridge, Mass.: Harvard Univ. Pr., 1971), pp. 248–49; Dworkin, "Paternalism," *Monist* 56 (1972): 65.

to a scheme of penalties that may give them a sufficient motive to avoid foolish actions."[13]

Arguments opposed to paternalism

Those impressed by Mill's position have offered three main arguments, beyond mere appeals to the principle of autonomy, in support of antipaternalism. The first argument is consequentialist: even limited paternalistic rules or polices can easily be abused and will inevitably lead to serious adverse consequences when put into practice. Those concerned about paternalism in government mention the dangers of incompetent and value-laden administrators, neglect of or failure of expertise in understanding individual and group needs, and political jockeying for power and position. They note that decisions by officials are often reached in ignorance and yet may have far-reaching consequences. Those concerned about paternalism in medicine cite abuses that may result from the latitude of judgment granted by paternalism to physicians or other medical professionals.

The second reason offered in defense of antipaternalism challenges Dworkin's claim that the rational individual informed of the risks and social pressures involved in community living would not object to a limited paternalism. As Mill repeatedly points out, the idea of "the informed rational individual" is often a mask for the will of a majority in society who may be unaffected, or the least affected, by paternalistic social policies. Also, many rational persons would be justifiably sceptical of the ability of others both to know their interests better than they would and to act so as to promote those interests. The rationale for paternalistic policies is often nothing but the acceptable or familiar and a corollary rejection of an alternative lifestyle or set of preferences that deviates from one's own. It is precisely in circumstances under which paternalism would be most likely to flourish, such as the context of the patient-physician relationship, that antipaternalists are most reluctant to believe that others would be in a position to protect them against themselves. For example, while arguing against paternalistic policies for the elderly, and while quoting Mill in his behalf, Thomas Halper writes as follows: "Though the aged citizen will not invariably perceive his

13. Rawls, *A Theory of Justice*, p. 249.

own self-interest, he will do so more often than will public officials or even family members, for only he can appreciate his desires, fears, needs, and perspectives with the unalloyed purity of an insider." [14] As antipaternalists see it, these individuals are in a position to ascertain their interests more competently than, for example, their family or their physicians; and thus at most we would be justified in making opportunities more readily available to persons to promote the interests we think they ought to promote. Educational interventions and incentives are acceptable to the antipaternalist; liberty-limitation is not.

Finally, an antipaternalist will recognize the practical wisdom and cautious foresight behind the social-insurance-policy justifications offered by Dworkin and Rawls, but will argue that the consent that these philosophers acknowledge to be given to authorities or to schemes of penalties renders this position libertarian rather than liberty-limiting, and thus deprives it of standing as a valid form of paternalism. Suppose, for example, that persons in an organized collection unit empower others to impose on them, under the appropriate conditions, schemes of involuntary commitment, extraordinary taxation on cigarettes, and health insurance penalties for accidents incurred in unnecessary high risk ventures. Whether implied consent or an explicit consent is involved makes no difference; the consent validates these schemes of intervention, and so robs them of standing as paternalistic. Such justifications are no more paternalistic in the eyes of an antipaternalist than the purchasing of a life insurance policy that demands annual payments one would not choose were it not for the security obtained by the purchase. If the social-insurance argument is among the strongest grounds in justification of paternalism, as Rawls and Dworkin seem to hold, then that position has a foundation in consent, and this alone is its justification, not an independent principle of paternalism. To take a simple example, as Don VanDeVeer has argued in another context, a physician cannot paternalistically interfere with a patient by withholding information if the patient has authorized the physician not

14. Thomas Halper, "Paternalism and the Elderly," in *Aging and the Elderly: Humanistic Perspectives in Gerontology*, ed. Stuart Spicker, Kathleen Woodward, and David D. Van Tassel (New York: Humanities Press, 1978), p. 323.

to disclose the information.[15] On the contrary, VanDeVeer argues, the physician would be guilty of noncompliance if he did not with hold.

These three arguments used by antipaternalists indicate that one major source of the difference between supporters and opponents of paternalism rests on the emphasis each places on capabilities for autonomous action by patients making "choices." Supporters of paternalism tend to cite examples of persons of diminished capacity, for example, persons lingering on kidney dialysis, chronic alcoholics, compulsive smokers, and seriously depressed suicidal patients. Opponents of paternalism cite examples of persons who are capable of autonomous choice, but have been socially restricted in exercising their capacities. Examples of this group include those involuntarily committed to institutions largely for eccentric behavior, prisoners not permitted to volunteer for risky research, and those who might rationally elect to refuse treatment in life-threatening circumstances.

One critical element of this controversy thus concerns the quality of consent or refusal by the persons whose liberty might be restricted by such policies. This problem directs our attention to the most important distinction yet encountered, that between paternalism that restricts substantially voluntary behaviors, commonly said to be *strong* paternalism, and paternalism that restricts substantially nonvoluntary behaviors, generally referred to as *weak* paternalism.

Strong and weak paternalism

Strong paternalism restricts information and overrides the informed and voluntary actions of individuals where information and actions significantly affect only the individuals themselves. For example, the strong paternalist would presumably restrict diagnostic information from a patient that might lead the patient to suicide and would intervene to stop attempts by antonomous agents to commit suicide.

Weak paternalism, by contrast, has been a far more popular theory in both law and moral philosophy. Indeed, it is the received view in contemporary moral philosophy. It holds that an indi-

15. Donald VanDeVeer, "The Contractual Argument for Withholding Medical Information," *Philosophy and Public Affairs* 9 (1980): 204.

vidual's self-regarding conduct can be restricted only when it is substantially nonvoluntary or substantially uninformed. Such cases involve some measure of voluntary and informed action, but the action must nonetheless be substantially nonvoluntary or uninformed. Being under the influence of psychotropic drugs, or in a uremic condition, or unable to grasp much of the language spoken in a hospital, or in paniful labor while delivering a child, or suffering from a blow on the head that affects memory and judgment are all medical situations that significantly compromise a patient's voluntariness or understanding. Yet patients in these situations may retain some capacity to make judgment and exhibit some capacity for voluntary action and consent. Drug addicts, the mentally ill, and patients with strongly conditioned habits can even be characterized by partial capacity and partial incapacity for long periods of time. Weak paternalism, then, holds that a person's autonomy or liberty may be limited because his or her capacity for autonomous action is severely restricted.

The analogy to the authority of a father from which the term "paternalism" is derived is useful for illustrating weak paternalism. Children of age ten, let us say, are not *non*autonomous. Rather, they commonly exhibit a limited or diminished autonomy (relative to some standard) owing to a limited capacity for making voluntary or informed decisions. These children are classified as minors and as legal incompetents, and their parents are empowered to override the "choices" of their children. Other groups besides children are similarly treated. For example, many mentally retarded persons are capable of some substantially informed and voluntary decisions and actions, such as whether to seek new employment. Yet these same persons may have severely limited capacities to process information and to make voluntary decisions when considering their medical treatment; thus, they can nonvoluntarily or uninformedly inflict harms "on themselves" partially as the result of their limited capacities. Weak paternalism holds that in cases where any person's capacity for voluntary action or informed judgment is analogously affected, so that it is partially voluntary or partially informed but substantially nonvoluntary or substantially uninformed, it is justified to override the person's choices and expressed wishes on grounds that someone else knows his interests better than he does himself and can protect him from harm *in his current condition*.

By almost anyone's standard, to allow persons to die or suffer

serious injury through decisions that are involuntary or question-
ably voluntary would be callous and uncaring; our natural sympathy
toward this viewpoint no doubt accounts for the broad support lav-
ished on weak paternalism. On the other hand, the intervention in
their lives is justified only if there is questionable voluntariness or
an information gap, not merely because of the dangerous or unreasonable character of their action. This requirement of weak paternalism paradoxically raises a question on which I shall concentrate for
the remainder of this essay: whether there is any truly significant
difference between weak paternalists and antipaternalists.

SIMILARITIES BETWEEN ANTIPATERNALISM AND WEAK PATERNALISM

Defenders of weak paternalism have generally thought antipaternalism to be a wholly indefensible and detestable doctrine—
especially when it prohibited beneficent medical interventions. Who,
after all, would not offer medical protection for defenseless leukemic
children, the mentally retarded, confused and frightened cardiac
patients, hope-exhausted and chronically depressed dialysis patients,
and those who have so little information about their case as to mis-
understand completely their situation? The answer, of course, is that
no caring and decent, sane person would leave such patients unpro-
tected. Weak paternalists have thus had a relatively easy time depicting antipaternalists as radicals in ethical theory who have been
carried away by the deceptive attractiveness of Mill's defense of
freedom or by some other defense of autonomy. Antipaternalists,
they suggest, mistakenly equate a successful rejection of *strong* paternalism with a successful wholesale rejection of all forms of
paternalism.

The weak paternalist thus may seem for two reasons to have
every advantage over the antipaternalist. First, many of the interventions defended by the weak paternalist are clearly justified and
are in the patients' best interest; yet antipaternalism apparently
must condemn them as unwarranted interferences with liberty. Second, weak paternalists can agree with all the arguments antipaternalists direct at strong paternalism, thus giving the appearance that
weak paternalism steers a moderate and reasonable course between
the two radical and excessive extremes of strong paternalism and
antipaternalism. If these contentions are sound, antipaternalists
are defending a detestable and confused position worthy of the pile

of discarded philosophical theories. But is the argument sound?

The strongly intuitive appeal of the beneficent interventions sketched above may seem decisive. If some forms of "paternalism" are clearly justified, then antipaternalism is just as clearly mistaken, and the problem of paternalism for ethical theory is reduced to that of deciding which form of paternalism is correct. That is, the problem is no longer whether paternalism is justified but merely the conditions under which paternalistic interventions are justified; we have only to choose between extensive or limited and between strong or weak forms of paternalism. Having so chosen, all that remains is to specify more precisely the conditions that legitimate one of these forms of paternalism.

One difficulty with this approach is that weak paternalism—the most popular and appealing account—may not be paternalism in any interesting sense. To be a distinct moral position, paternalism must embrace a liberty-limiting principle independent of Mill's harm principle. In a truly paternalistic theory, protecting an individual from harm caused by conditions beyond his or her knowledge and voluntary control is not a reason for liberty limitation or autonomy restriction. Rather, the "action" performed and the resultant harm must be self-caused, under a theory of causation and responsibility that makes the action or occurrence that person's responsibility and not a mere consequence of causes beyond the person's control. This matter is of paramount importance. If the real underlying justification for a so-called paternalistic intervention is to protect a person from causes that are not of his or her own making or responsibility, then the intervention in question is not paternalistic in the antipaternalists' sense, and indeed is but an extended form of Mill's harm principle. The antipaternalist will maintain that because weak paternalistic cases involve externally caused limitations, weak paternalism does not rest on independent liberty-limiting grounds and can no longer be distinguished from antipaternalism.

It seems clear from literature expressing the pro-paternalistic position that there is a significant confusion of definitions, constituting a considerable conceptual but not moral gulf between paternalists and antipaternalists. Many conceptions of "justified paternalism" are by definition not paternalism at all for the antipaternalist. When Michael Bayles writes that the only acceptable paternalism is one that "restricts a person's actions only if they are *involuntary* and injurious,"[16] and when Rawls writes that the authorization of paternalistic interventions given to another comes "into effect only when we cannot look after our own good" and that "paternalistic intervention must be justified by the evident failure or absence of reason and will,"[17] they are writing about a "paternalism" antipaternalists do not recognize as deserving of the label. (Otherwise the antipaternalist would be some form of paternalist.) Indeed Rawls's paternalism is morally indistinguishable in all important respects from Mill's antipaternalism, for both spring from similar reservations about human liberty and state control and rely on similar conceptions of autonomy.

The antipaternalist, then, does not deny that the interventions or acts of withholding information sanctioned by reasonable forms of weak paternalism are justified. On the contrary, antipaternalists agree that such interventions are often justified, and it would appear that they invoke justifying reasons identical to those invoked by weak paternalists. These reasons turn on the need to protect the patient from nonautonomously produced harm. In short, the antipaternalist too believes that an intervention can be justified when it protects a patient against harmful consequences of substantially nonvoluntary or uninformed behavior, a position that appears indistinguishable from weak paternalism.

Mill's Proviso

A directly related issue was addressed by Mill in *On Liberty*, and was resolved along essentially similar lines. He took up the issue of justifying *temporary* interventions that limit liberty. Sissela Bok and others have explicitly referred to such temporary restraint as paternalistic,[18] and Mill is sometimes wrongly condemned as inconsistently sanctioning paternalism. Mill's contention is that a person ignorant of a potential danger that might befall him may

16. Michael Bayles, "Criminal Paternalism," in J. Pennock and J. Chapman, eds., *The Limits of Law*, Nomos XV (Chicago: Atherton, 1974), p. 179 (italics added). A similar view based on "incompetence" as a condition of paternalism is found in Jeffrie Murphy, "Incompetence and Paternalism," *Archiv für Rechts und Sozial-Philosophie* 60 (1974), p. 466.

17. Rawls, *A Theory of Justice*, pp. 249f (italics added).

18. See Sissela Bok, "Lying to Children: The Risks of Paternalism," *Hastings Center Report* (June, 1978): 10–13.

justifiably be restrained, so long as the coercion is temporary and serves only to render the person informed and of voluntary ability. Thereafter the person should be free to choose whatever course he or she wishes. Mill did not regard this temporary intervention as a "real infringement" of liberty, and thus did not view it as paternalistic; for if a person is uninformed about certain dangers, he or she is not acting at all in regard to the danger posed by the situation. The person needs protection from something which is *not himself or herself*, not his or her intended action, not in any relevant sense of his or her own making. Mill thus holds that once the person has been adequately informed and understands the dangers of, for example, an unsafe bridge, he should be left free to traverse it should he so desire.

Regarding the charge that Mill inconsistently espouses paternalism through this example, it is worth noting how easily Mill can be conceptually switched from the role of the classical antipaternalist to a weak paternalist merely by shifting the definition of paternalism from that used by antipaternalists to that used by weak paternalists. Mill justifies restraint of a substantially nonvoluntary action in order to protect a person against his own actions, as the above example certifies. His position thus can be validly described as "paternalistic" as many weak paternalists use the term. However, whether it be labelled as weak paternalism or as antipaternalism, I shall hereafter refer to his justification of temporary intervention as "Mill's proviso." The antipaternalist attempts to handle all problems of paternalism in principle by Mill's proviso: once an agent ignorant of or unable to comprehend critical information or less than adequately voluntary is adequately informed (assuming disclosure and comprehension are possible and assuming the person is able to act on the information) and in a condition of adequate voluntariness, the decision should rest with the agent.

Application of these arguments to strong paternalism

The challenge issued to the distinction between antipaternalism and weak paternalism by the above arguments can be reduced to the following simple terms: since by definition weak paternalism applies only to substantially nonvoluntary or uninformed persons, and since by definition such persons are substantially nonautonomous, the antipaternalist will not object to beneficent interventions that do not violate autonomy. Strong paternalism, of course, does involve interventions that override autonomy, and thus appears to be the only striking and interesting form of paternalism. Accordingly, having challenged the distinction between weak paternalism and antipaternalism, we should now consider whether similar considerations vitiate the distinction between strong paternalism and weak paternalism, thus effectively collapsing all forms of paternalism and antipaternalism.

The distinction between weak and strong paternalists, I suggest, is threatened by the same difficulties that render problematic the distinction between weak paternalism and antipaternalism. For it is not implausible to suppose that the strong paternalist, the weak paternalist, and the antipaternalist will ultimately agree that the fundamental consideration that makes legitimate apparently paternalistic interventions is the substantial nonautonomy of a particular agent. Consider cases in which strong paternalists presumably would intervene, while antipaternalists and weak paternalists would not. The weak paternalist and the antipaternalist will regard the strong paternalist as one who overrides autonomy in these cases. Yet it is not likely in the most important and controversial cases that the so-called "strong paternalist" will accept this description and agree that the patients are correctly described as autonomous. Instead, in justifying an intervention, the "strong paternalist" will refer to factors influencing the patient's judgment such as stress, inexperience, severe pain, and lack of appreciation of the future. There will seldom if ever be a naked appeal to a beneficent paternalistic interest, unqualified by considerations of limited capacity or knowledge. Thus, even though the so-called strong paternalist will often be depicted as overriding autonomy, in fact the reason invoked to justify intervention is not paternalistic, for the patients are not regarded as adequately autonomous.

Accordingly, the justifying reasons used by an alleged strong paternalist may turn out to be similar in kind to those used by weak paternalists and antipaternalists. This justification will again appeal to inordinately powerful psychological or situational factors that render a person substantially nonautonomous. If this analysis is correct, then when we turn to the most controversial cases of intervention, we should expect the disagreement between strong paternalists and their opponents to focus on empirically based theories of voluntariness and information, and to a lesser degree on moral views about the degree to which we are to respect these qualities when they are present. This outcome is not as paradoxical as it might at first seem, for we have long known that significantly different psychiatric theories, for example, result in significantly different views about how to handle patients.

The upshot of this line of thought is that many interesting issues masked under the label of paternalism turn on disagreements about conditions of voluntariness and information possession—not on commitments to liberty-limiting principles independent of the harm principle. To the extent this argument is correct, physicians are not paternalistic in their treatment of patients merely because they override the apparent choices or desires of patients. If they attempt to justify their intervention by appeal to the compromised character of the patient in the circumstances, the intervention is at least not intended as paternalistic. In short, the critical disagreements turn out to be disagreements about the compromised character of the patient and what that compromised condition entails—not disagreements about paternalism itself.

It must not be supposed, however, that there cannot or never will be cases of strong paternalism, where purely paternalistic grounds are invoked for an intervention. The National Park Service of the U.S. Department of the Interior, for example, regularly makes sweeping restrictions on the activities in which visitors to national parks may engage, though to our knowledge there is not even an implicit consent of the governed to these policies.[19] Thus there obviously can be cases of pure strong paternalism. However, we are inclined to think that major interventions will generally be regarded by thoughtful paternalists as unjustified.

Many cases in medicine involving the invocation of a physician's therapeutic privilege superficially seem to perpetuate strong paternalism as a major theoretical problem. In my judgment, however, it is more likely that such cases of withholding information will be widely regarded by physicians and philosophers alike as simply unwarranted violations of patient autonomy. However, the point of the argument in this section has not been that there can be no strong paternalism, but rather that the interesting and urgent problems of

19. Already famous for its restrictions on rafting, mountain climbing, and hang gliding, the NPS recently provoked a controversy by restricting environmentalists from attempting to save burros in the Grand Canyon on grounds that the persons descending into the canyon would be seriously endangering themselves. See *Parade Magazine*, April 27, 1980, p. 4.

intervention by authorities turn more on issues of how to understand and treat substantially nonautonomous agents, not on paternalistic issues.

ADEQUATE VOLUNTARINESS AND ADEQUATE COMPREHENSION

Mill's proviso has been invoked to bring the arguments of weak paternalists, strong paternalists, and antipaternalists to the uniform conclusion that in cases where we are unsure whether a person's actions are sufficiently voluntary or their judgment adequately informed, it is justifiable to intervene temporarily. Still, what should be done in the hard cases of actions that are partially voluntary and partially nonvoluntary, partially informed and partially ignorant, where an informed and voluntary state cannot be brought about? These cases might involve mental retardation, immaturity in children of advanced ages, false beliefs that cannot be overcome, ongoing psychotic compulsion, or repeated tendencies to suicide from depression. Perhaps all such situations should be modeled on Mill's proviso so that the factors limiting voluntariness or comprehension are also those that (at least partially) justify protecting persons from harm caused by unforeseen conditions. The intervention would then have plausible claim to moral justification based on an extension of the harm principle: the person is protected from harms produced by causes beyond his or her knowledge and voluntary control. By invoking Mill's proviso, we justifiably protect persons from harm that might result directly from their drunkenness, retardation, uremic condition, drug state, pain state, etc., so long as they are affected by their limiting conditions. However, once adequately informed of the dangers of his or her action and once situated so that voluntary choice is meaningfully possible, the person cannot justifiably be restrained.

Certain classes of retarded persons provide a useful example where restrictions are sometimes justified even in the eyes of antipaternalists. Retarded persons with minimal language skills are often not capable of voluntary choices concerning their medical treatment. Interventions in their affairs may protect them from injury or exploitation, and such intervention is justified. Degrees of control, voluntariness, and comprehension rest on a multi-level continuum for the retarded, and it will often prove difficult or impossible to ascertain whether their choices and actions are substantially informed and voluntary; however, this will not alter the principle that a person may justifiably be protected against harmful consequences of self-regarding behavior when that behavior is relevantly nonvoluntary or uninformed and is caused by conditions beyond the person's knowledge and control.

The interesting problem of strong and weak paternalism thus rests on a set of issues and moral problems quite different from those discussed in the literature on the subject. Most who have addressed these issues do not seem to have appreciated the real substance of the problem. The issues generated by so-called weak paternalism apparently have nothing to do with paternalism as such or with the justification of a "paternalistic principle." Indeed, on the analysis offered here most forms of strong and weak paternalism are not paternalistic, or at least they cannot be differentiated in practice from antipaternalism, and so present an utterly uninteresting alternative to antipaternalism. It only clouds the issue to speak, as does H. Tristram Engelhardt, Jr., for example, of "a paternalism required because of the intrusions of a disease" when a patient's capacity for autonomy is overwhelmed by the ravages of disease. Englehardt maintains that "the more the patient is overwhelmed by the disease process . . . the easier it is to justify a physician's paternalism."[20] This comment of course mirrors the same conceptual problem as the earlier quotations from Rawls and others that we encountered in discussing weak paternalism. If the arguments I have advanced are correct, however, all these views are conceptually (though not morally) misleading. It would be more accurate to say that the more a disease affects voluntariness and comprehension the easier it is to justify a nonpaternalistic intervention, or perhaps an intervention *simpliciter*; for the issues of paternalism by definition involve a conflict between beneficence and autonomy, and, accordingly, are relevant to the limitation of liberty.

How, then, can we set about to resolve the major controversies over so-called "paternalistic" intervention with substantially nonvoluntary behaviors? First, we need a set of standards to determine the logical and empirical conditions under which a person is behaving in a substantially voluntary and informed manner. Second, we need to specify the moral conditions under which it is justified to limit substantially nonvoluntary and uninformed conduct through

20. H. Tristram Engelhardt, Jr., "Rights and Responsibilities of Patients and Physicians" in *Medical Treatment of the Dying*, eds., Michael D. Bayles and Dallas M. High (Cambridge, Mass.: Schenkman, 1978), pp. 18–19.

"authoritative" interventions into self-regarding conduct. The first issue is conceptual and empirical, the second moral (but not paternalistic). For moral philosophy, law, and social policy, the issue of theoretical and practical importance about paternalism is the second, that of specifying the conditions, if any, under which a person's action or decision is to be respected and honored even though the action or decision is substantially nonvoluntary or the person is uninformed. If a mildly retarded man refuses a surgical procedure whose real importance he appears not to appreciate, or a 17-year-old minor refuses a fourth kidney transplant that offers an excellent match because she is "tired of transplants that fail," shall we or shall we not respect and honor their "decisions?"

A comprehensive theory of the sort we are proposing would be enormously complex, making demands well beyond our present knowledge. The theory would have to detail the degree to which conditions of stress, pain, psychosis, intelligence, etc., affect voluntariness and information-processing, as well as the relevance of such effects to the way in which intervention is justified. No doubt we shall not possess such a comprehensive theory for some time, but we can at least begin to address the right issues and develop elements of the theory. Not to be neglected is the extent to which these issues are empirical. Whereas an account of the nature of voluntary and cognitive abilities or human action generally is inherently philosophical, the extent to which such voluntariness is impaired is an empirical and not a philosophical problem. A sophisticated solution to this empirical problem must figure centrally in any worthy philosophical theory of justified "paternalistic" intervention.

References

Index

References

CASE CITATIONS

Application of the President and Directors of Georgetown College, 331 F. 2d 1000 (D. C. Cir. 1964), *cert. denied*, 377 U. S. 978 (1964).

Canterbury v. Spence, 464 F. 2d 772 (D.C. Cir. 1972).

Defunis v. Odegaard, 94 S. Ct. 1704 (1974).

Prince v. Massachusetts, 321 U. S. 158 (1944).

State v. Garber, 197 Kan. 567, 419 P. 2d 896 (1966).

Superintendent of Belchertown v. Saikewicz, 373 Mass. 728, 370 N. E. 2d 417 at 427 (1977).

Wisconsin v. Yoder et al., 406 U. S. 205 (1972) (Douglas, J., dissenting).

BIBLIOGRAPHY

Arendt, Hannah. *The Human Condition*. Garden City: Doubleday, 1959.

Arrow, Kenneth. "Gifts and Exchanges." *Philosophy and Public Affairs* 1 (1972): 343–62.

Baskin, Stuart J. "State Intrusion into Family Affairs: Justifications and Limitations." *Stanford Law Review* 26 (1974): 1383–409.

Bayles, Michael D. "Criminal Paternalism." In *The Limits of Law*, edited by James R. Pennock and John W. Chapman, pp. 174–88. Chicago: Lieber-Atherton, 1974.

Biró, András. "The Nurturing Forest." *Ceres* 8 (March/April, 1975): 4.

Blackstone, William T., Jr., ed. *Philosophy and Environmental Crisis*. Athens: Univ. of Georgia Pr., 1974.

Bok, Sissela. "Lying to Children: The Risks of Paternalism." *Hastings Center Report* 8 (June, 1978): 10–13.

Boulding, Kenneth. *The Meaning of the Twentieth Century*. New York: Harper, 1964.

Brennan, Joseph G. *Ethics and Morals*. New York: Harper, 1973.

Buchanan, Allen. "Medical Paternalism." *Philosophy and Public Affairs* 7 (1978): 370–90.

Burnet, John. *Early Greek Philosophy*. 3d ed. London: A. C. Black, 1920.

Cohen, Morris R. *Reason and Nature*. New York: Harcourt, 1931.

Cohen, M. R.; Nagel, T.; and Scanlon, T., eds. *The Rights and Wrongs of Abortion*. Princeton: Princeton Univ. Pr., 1974.

Downie, R. S., and Telfer, E. *Respect for Persons*. London: Allen and Unwin, 1969.

Dworkin, Gerald. "Acting Freely." *Nous* 4 (1970): 367–83.

———. "Non-neutral Principles." *Journal of Philosophy* 71 (1974): 491–506.

———. "Paternalism." *Monist* 56 (1972): 64–84.

Dworkin, Gerald; Bermant, Gordon; and Brown, Peter G., eds. *Markets and Morals*. New York: Hemisphere Publishing, 1977.

Eckholm, Erik P. "Losing Ground: Impinging Ecological Disaster." *The Humanist* 33 (Nov./Dec., 1973): 17–21.

Edelstein, Ludwig. *Ancient Medicine: Selected Papers of Ludwig Edelstein*. Edited by Owsei Temkin and C. Lillian Temkin. Baltimore: Johns Hopkins Univ. Pr., 1967.

Ehrlich, Paul R. *The Population Bomb*. New York: Ballantine, 1968.

Englehardt, H. Tristram, Jr. "Rights and Responsibilities of Patients and Physicians." In *Medical Treatment of the Dying*, edited by Michael D. Bayles and Dallas M. High, pp. 9–21. Cambridge, Mass.: Schenkman, 1978.

Feinberg, Joel. "Absurd Self-fulfillment: An Essay on the Merciful Perversity of the Gods." In *Time and Cause, Essays Presented to Richard Taylor*, edited by Peter van Inwagen, pp. 255–81. Dortrecht, The Netherlands: Reidel, 1979.

———. "Freedom and Behavioral Control." In *The Encyclopedia of Bioethics*, edited by Warren T. Reich. Vol. 1, 93–101. New York: The Free Press, 1978.

———. "Legal Paternalism." *Canadian Journal of Philosophy* 1 (1971): 105–24.

———. "The Nature and Value of Rights." *The Journal of Value Inquiry* 4 (1970): 263–67.

Fletcher, Joseph F. *Morals and Medicine*. Princeton: Princeton Univ. Pr., 1954.

Fox, Donald T., ed. *The Role of Law in Population Planning.* Dobbs Ferry, N.Y.: Oceana Publications, 1972.

Frankena, William K. "On Saying the Ethical Thing." *Proceedings and Addresses of the American Philosophical Association* 39 (1966): 21–42.

Gert, Bernard M., and Culver, Charles. "Paternalistic Behavior." *Philosophy and Public Affairs* 6 (1976): 45–57.

Giannella, Donald. "Religious Liberty, Nonestablishment, and Doctrinal Development." Pt. I, "The Religious Liberty Guarantee." *Harvard Law Review* 80 (1967): 1381–431.

Glover, Jonathan. *Causing Death and Saving Lives.* New York: Penguin, 1977.

Greene, Ward. "Triage." *New York Times Magazine*, Jan. 5, 1975, pp. 9–11, 44–45, 51.

Halper, Thomas. "Paternalism and the Elderly." In *Aging and the Elderly: Humanistic Perspectives in Gerontology*, edited by Stuart F. Spicker, Kathleen M. Woodward, and David D. Van Tassel, pp. 321–39. New York: Humanities Press, 1978.

Hardin, Garrett. *Exploring New Ethics for Survival: The Voyage of the Spaceship Beagle.* New York: Penguin, 1973.

———. "Lifeboat Ethics: The Case Against Helping the Poor." *Psychology Today* 8 (1974): 38–43.

———. "Living on a Lifeboat." *Bioscience* 25 (1974): 561–68.

Harkness, Georgia. *The Sources of Western Morality.* New York: Scribner's, 1954.

Hart, H. L. A. *Law, Liberty, and Morality.* Stanford: Stanford Univ. Pr., 1963.

———. "Rawls on Liberty and Its Priority." *University of Chicago Law Review* 40 (1973): 534–55.

Heilbroner, Robert. *An Inquiry into the Human Prospect.* New York: Norton, 1974.

Henley, Kenneth. "The Authority to Educate." In *Having Children: Philosophical and Legal Reflections on Parenthood*, edited by Onora O'Neill and William Ruddick, pp. 254–64. New York: Oxford Univ. Pr., 1979.

H. R. Doc. No. 139. Message from the President of the United States Relative to Population Growth. July 21, 1969. 91st Cong. 1st Session 3.

Huxley, Aldous. *Brave New World Revisited*. New York: Harper, 1965.

Jonas, Hans. *Philosophical Essays*. Englewood Cliffs, N.J.: Prentice-Hall, 1974.

Kant, Immanuel. *Lectures on Ethics*. Trans. by Louis Infield. New York: Century, 1930.

Katz, R. L. "Informed Consent: Is It Bad Medicine?" *Western Journal of Medicine* 126 (1977): 426–28.

Kierkegaard, Søren. *Fear and Trembling and The Sickness Unto Death*. Trans. by Walter Lowrie. Garden City, N.Y.: Doubleday, 1954.

Labby, Daniel H., ed. *Life or Death: Ethics and Options*. Seattle: Univ. of Washington Pr., 1968.

Laslett, Peter; Runciman, Walter G.; and Skinner, Quentin, eds. *Philosophy, Politics and Society*. 4th Series. Oxford: Blackwell, 1967.

Lecky, W. E. H. *History of European Morals from Augustus to Charlemagne*. 11 ed. 2 vols. London: Longmans Green, 1894.

Lewis, Clarence I. *Analysis of Knowledge and Valuation*. La Salle, Ill.: Open Court, 1946.

Locke, John. *Second Treatise of Civil Government*. Oxford: B. Blackwell, 1946.

Loftus, Elizabeth F., and Friess, James F. "Informed Consent May Be Hazardous to Your Health." *Science*, April 6, 1979, p. 11.

Mayer, Jean. "Toward A Non-Malthusian Population Policy." *Milbank Memorial Fund Quarterly* 47 (1969): 340–53.

McCormick, Richard A. *Ambiguity in Moral Choice*. Milwaukee: Marquette Univ. Pr., 1977.

McKean, Roland. "Growth Versus No-growth: An Evaluation." *Daedalus* 102, No. 4 (Fall, 1973), pp. 207–27.

Meadows, Dennis L.; Meadows, Donella H.; Randers, Jørgen and Behrens, William W., III. *The Limits to Growth: A Report for the Club of Rome's Project on the Predicament of Mankind*. Washington, D.C.: Potomac Press, 1972.

Mesarovic, M., and Pestel, E. *Mankind at the Turning Point*. New York: E. P. Dutton, 1974.

Milhaven, J. G. *Toward a New Catholic Morality*. Garden City, N.Y.: Image Books, 1972.

Mill, John Stuart. *On Liberty*. Edited by Gertrude Himmelfarb. New York: Penguin, 1974.

———. *Principles of Political Economy*. 2 vols. New York: Kelley, 1900.

Mishan, E. J. "Ills, Bads, and Disamenities: The Wages of Growth." *Daedalus* 102, no. 4 (Fall, 1973), pp. 63–87.

Mortimer, R. C. *Christian Ethics*. London: Hutchinsons' Univ. Library, 1950.

Murphy, Jeffrie. "Incompetence and Paternalism." *Archiv für Rechts und Sozial-Philosophie* 60 (1974): 465–86.

Odum, Eugene. "Preventive Law." *Life (Legal Information for Environmentalists)* 1 (1975): 1, 3, 4.

Olsen, E. O. "Some Theorems in the Theory of Efficient Transfers." *Journal of Political Economy* 79 (1971): 166–76.

Olsen, Mancur. "Introduction" to "The No-growth Society." *Daedalus* 102, no. 4 (Fall, 1973), pp. 1–13.

Painter, Hal. *Mark, I Love You*. New York: Simon & Schuster, 1968.

Patten, B. M., and Stump, W. "Death Related to Informed Consent." *Texas Medicine* 74 (1978): 49–50.

Perry, Ralph B. *Realms of Value*. Cambridge, Mass.: Harvard Univ. Pr., 1954.

Racklin, H. *Introduction to Modern Behaviorism*. San Francisco: W. H. Freeman, 1979.

Raphael, D. D., ed. *British Moralists, 1650–1800*. Oxford: Clarendon Pr., 1969.

Rawls, John. *A Theory of Justice*. Cambridge, Mass.: Harvard Univ. Pr., 1971.

Richards, Howard. "Productive Justice." Paper read at the American Philosophical Association. Eastern Division, New York, Dec. 26–29, 1974.

Roberts, John C. "Civil Restraint, Mental Illness and the Right to Treatment." *Yale Law Journal* 77 (1967): 87–116.

Rolston, Holmes, III. "Is There An Ecological Ethic?" *Ethics* 85 (1975): 93–109.

Ross, William David. *The Right and the Good*. Oxford: Clarendon Pr., 1930.

Savage, M. J. *The Morals of Evolution*. Boston: G. H. Ellis, 1880.

Schweitzer, Albert. *Civilization and Ethics*. 3rd ed. London: A. C. Black, 1949.

Schumacher, E. F. *Small is Beautiful: Economics as if People Mattered*. New York: Harper, 1975.

Scitovsky, Tibor. *The Joyless Economy*. New York: Oxford Univ. Pr., 1976.

Sidgwick, Henry. *The Ethics of T. H. Green, H. Spencer, and J. Martineau*. London: Macmillan, 1902.

—————. *The Methods of Ethics*. 7th ed. London: Macmillan, 1930.

—————. *Outlines of the History of Ethics*. London: Macmillan, 1931.

Slater, Philip. *Earthwalk*. New York: Anchor, 1974.

Spencer, Herbert. *The Data of Ethics*. New York: A. L. Burt, n.d.

Stone, Christopher. "Should Trees Have Standing? Toward Legal Rights for Natural Objects." *Southern California Law Review* 45 (1972): 450–501.

Szasz, Thomas S. "Involuntary Mental Hospitalization: A Crime Against Humanity." In *Contemporary Issues in Bioethics*, edited by Tom L. Beauchamp and Leroy Walters, pp. 551–57. Belmont, Ca.: Dickenson, 1978.

Thomas, George F. *Christian Ethics and Moral Philosophy*. New York: Scribners, 1955.

Titmuss, Richard. *The Gift Relationship*. New York: Random House, 1972.

Tullock, Gordon. "Inheritance Justified." *Journal of Law and Economics* 14 (1971): 465–74.

—————. *The Logic of the Law*. New York: Basic Books, 1971.

U Thant. *Declaration on Population: The World Leaders' Statement*, Studies in Family Planning No. 26 (Jan., 1968): 1–3.

VanDeVeer, Donald. "The Contractual Argument for Withholding Medical Information." *Philosophy and Public Affairs* 9 (1980): 198–205.

Veatch, Robert M., and Tai, Ernest. "Talking About Death: Patterns of Lay and Professional Change." *The Annals of the American Academy of Political and Social Science* 447 (Jan., 1980): 29–45.

Warren, Mary A. "On the Moral and Legal Status of Abortion." *Monist* 57 (1973): 43–61.

Wasserstrom, Richard. *Philosophy and Social Issues: Five Studies*. Notre Dame, Ind.: Univ. of Notre Dame Pr., 1980.

Wisdom, John. *Problems of Mind and Matter*. Cambridge: Cambridge Univ. Pr., 1934.

Zeckhauser, Richard. "The Risks of Growth." *Daedalus* 102, No. 4 (Fall, 1973), pp. 103–18.

Index

Abortion, 2, 3, 4, 8; absolutely or prima facie wrong, 9; and amniocentesis, 83–84; ancient proscription based on father's right to offspring, 13, 15; Aristotles's view of, 14; difficult case of, 19; Frankena's view of, 29; legality of, 35; population control measure, 38; rule and act utilitarian view of, 24–25

Affirmative action, programs of, 54–56, 71–77

Amish religion, 106–7, 109–10. See also State v. Garber

Amendment: Equal Rights, 63; First, 106; Fourteenth, 108

Antipaternalism, 128, 131–32, 133, 134, 137

Aristotle, 14, 31, 49–50, 117, 120–21

Arrow, Kenneth, 80, 85–86. See also Singer, Peter; Titmuss, Richard

Assimilationist ideal, 62–63, 65, 67–69, 70

Autonomy, 114–16, 134. See also Self-determination

Bathrooms, segregation of, 59, 60, 61

Beneficence, 123, 126, 128, 130

Blackstone, William T., 45

Blood, donation and sale of. See Arrow, Kenneth; Singer, Peter; Titmuss, Richard

Bok, Sissela, 137

Brennan, Joseph, 32–33

Buchanan, Allen, 125

Burger, Warren, 106–9

Canterbury v. Spence, 126

Children: 101, 110–12, 118, 134. See also Rights, of children

Choices, 79, 81, 83–90, 91–93, 94–96. See also Freedom

Christianity, opposition of, 12, 17

Clarke, Samuel, 23

Cohen, Morris R., 20–21, 29–30

Comprehension, inadequacy of, 142

Conflicts, between adults and children, 101–12

Consent, 124–25, 129, 132, 133

Contraception, 4, 8–9, 19; distribution of IUD's and condoms, 44; information on, 38; preventing bodily human life, 2, 40; and tax incentives, 41

Costs, of decision-making, xvi, 82–83

Double effect, doctrine of, 18–19

Dworkin, Gerald, xvi, 125–26, 130–32

Economy, growth, 44–47, 48–49, 52–53

Economy, no-growth, 46, 48, 50–51, 52

Edelstein, Ludwig, 9, 11, 13, 15

Education, 76–77, 103–4, 106–7, 109–10. See also State v. Garber; Wisconsin v. Yoder

Euthanasia, 2–3, 18–19, 20, 29

Ehrlich, Paul, 40–41

Engelhardt, H. Tristram, Jr., 142

Fletcher, Joseph F., 9, 17

Freedom, 39, 40, 44, 125, 126–27

Government, paternalism by, 131

Happiness, 21, 39, 46–47

Hardin, Garrett, 41–42

Hart, H. L. A., 91, 125, 129

Henley, Kenneth, 113, 118

Hippocratic Oath, 11, 13, 14, 15, 20

Ideals, for society, 62, 63–64, 65–70, 112

Income, personal, xv, 46–47, 51–52

Interests: of children, 119; of patients, 124, 131–32; and rights, 99–101, 103

Intervention, of a temporary medical kind, 138–41

Iowa, Painter custody case in, 110–12

John Howie, Associate Professor of Philosophy at Southern Illinois University, Carbondale, Illinois, received his Ph.D. degree from Boston University. He has co-edited two books, *Contemporary Studies in Philosophical Idealism* and *The Wisdom of William Ernest Hocking*, and has published essays in *The Philosophical Forum*, *Stylus*, *Religious Studies*, and *Indian Philosophical Quarterly*.